DATE DUE

MAR 30	MAY 0 4 1994	
SEP 11	FEB 2 7 1996	
APR 24	JAN 1 9 1998	
DEC 28		
SEP 22		
OCT 24		
MAR 20		
MAY 3		

Public Library
St. Joseph, Michigan

1. Books may be kept two weeks and may be renewed once for the same period, except 7 day books and magazines.

2. A fine is charged for each day a book is not returned according to the above rule. No book will be issued to any person incurring such a fine until it has been paid.

3. All injuries to books beyond reasonable wear and all losses shall be made good to the satisfaction of the Librarian.

4. Each borrower is held responsible for all books charged on his card and for all fines accruing on the same.

LIE DETECTORS

Other books by Eugene B. Block

LIE DETECTORS:

Their History and Use,

EUGENE B. BLOCK

David McKay Company, Inc.

NEW YORK

Library of Congress Cataloging in Publication Data

Block, Eugene B
    Lie detectors.

    Includes index.
    1. Lie detectors and detection—History.
    2. Lie detectors and detection—Case studies.
    I. Title.
    HV8078.B55   364.12′8   77-8887
    ISBN 0-679-50755-0

Extracted material on pages 21–22 reprinted by permission
of The Yale Law Journal Company and Fred B. Rothman & Company
from *The Yale Law Journal*, Vol. 70, pp. 694ff.

10 9 8 7 6 5 4 3 2 1

Manufactured in the United States of America

To Ruth,
with love

CONTENTS

In Conclusion

ACKNOWLEDGMENTS

The author, with a deep sense of gratitude, expresses his profound thanks to the many people throughout the country whose kindly help made this book possible. They include:

Mrs. Marjorie P. Block, Kentfield, California
Chief of Police Richard Young, Alameda, Californa
Richard Zevitz, Chief Parole Officer, San Francisco, California
Donald Hesse, San Francisco, California
W. Lee Clingan, Downey, California
Deputy District Attorney Michael Coleman, Concord, California
Stephen J. Long, San Francisco, California
Samuel Lister, Dept. of Justice, Sacramento, California
Charles S. Pizzo, Esq., Phoenix, Arizona
Mark B. Halverson, Citrus Heights, California
Jerry Littman, Supt. of Justice, Sacramento, California
Jessie W. Murphy, Circuit Court, Pinellas County, Florida
Ivan A. Wemhoff, Chicago, Illinois
Clarence M. Kelley, Director FBI, Washington, D.C.
S.F. O'Donnell, New Scotland Yard, London, England
J. Nepote, Secretary-General Interpol, St. Cloud, France
Dr. Bernard L. Diamond, Ross, California
Bradford E. Block, Esq., Chicago, Illinois
Mrs. Alma Compton, University of California, Berkeley, California
Gene Miller, Miami, Florida
Leonard H. Harrelson, Chicago, Illinois
George W. Harmon, San Francisco, California
Judge Paul A. Dorf, Baltimore, Maryland
Lieutenant Albert E. Riedel, Walnut Creek, California
Rep. Philip Burton, Washington, D.C.
George S. Block, San Francisco, California
Joseph Henderson, Kansas City, Missouri
Charles W. Block, San Mateo, California
Doug Clarke, Fort Worth, Texas
The late Dr. Ludwig Rosenstein, San Francisco, California
Lieutenant L.T. Riegel, State Police, Milwaukie, Oregon

The author apologizes to any others whose names may have been inadvertently omitted.

PART ONE

History
and
Precedent

CHAPTER

1

Jail Doors Are Opened

For many months the case of Ervin Byrd, a luckless 34-year-old black, was a cause célèbre in Fort Worth, Texas. Byrd had spent his youth working on a farm in Louisiana. His parents, poor but proud, taught their seven children respect for the law, and Ervin vowed to live an honest and upright life. His high standards were to make his later experience all the more difficult to endure, for he had faith in the integrity of government and in those whose duty it was to enforce the law.

In time Byrd left the family farm and moved to Texas, where he was told jobs were plentiful and wages good. Striking out boldly for himself, he reached Fort Worth, where he found employment as a truck driver for a drug distributing firm. The pay was only fair, but by frugal living he was able to support himself and put a little money aside. Byrd had a special motivation to save his money—he wanted to marry. And several months later he did just that.

The young couple was happy; they had a home, a cheap car, and enough money for an occasional night out at a moderately priced restaurant or local movie house. Neither Byrd nor his bride dreamed that their happy, placid life would soon be rocked by disaster. The blow came on a grim night in August 1965 after two Fort Worth service station employees walked into police headquarters to report that they had been held up and robbed of $5,000 by a lone bandit. "And we're pretty sure we know exactly who did it," one of the men told the desk sergeant.

The supposed victim said he recognized the robber as a young black man who was an occasional customer at the station. He named Ervin Byrd and told the officer where he lived.

Byrd gasped in astonishment and horror when officers called at his poorly furnished home and told him he was under arrest for robbery. "I don't know what you're talking about," he exclaimed. "I don't know a thing about a gas station holdup, and I certainly didn't do it. Test me on a lie detector, and I'll prove I'm innocent."

"Don't be in such a hurry about a lie detctor," the arresting officers replied. "First we want you to stand in a line-up and let us find out what's what."

Still protesting his innocence, the unfortunate Byrd was locked in a cell for several hours. Finally, he was told to come out and stand in a line-up with five other prisoners. His two accusers were then brought from an adjoining room and instructed to point out the man they believed had committed the holdup.

Without a moment's hesitation they pointed at Byrd. "That's him," they chorused. "We're sure."

Byrd was led back to his cell; his continued pleas for a polygraph test went unheeded. Without funds to engage a lawyer, he begged for an early trial. No one seemed interested, and despite statutes guaranteeing prompt trials for the accused, Byrd continued to languish in jail while his distraught wife vainly sought to borrow enough money from friends to hire counsel.

Not until December 23, nearly four months after Byrd's arrest, did the case come before the Tarrant County Grand Jury, which returned an indictment charging Byrd with armed robbery. The case dragged into the new year. On January 4, District Judge Byron Matthews appointed attorney J. Harlon Fleming to represent Byrd without fee. The accused man was elated.

Fleming, an able and tireless lawyer, talked with Byrd in jail and was soon convinced that the man was being persecuted.

Realizing his responsibility as an officer of the court, Fleming decided to conduct an investigation of his own. What he uncovered was startling, and only as a result of his efforts did the wheels of justice begin to turn.

It did not take Fleming long to decide that the story of the robbery was a hoax. He was convinced that the two gas station employees had deliberately concocted the holdup report to hide their own embezzlement from their employers. This belief was bolstered by the lawyer's discovery that, on a previous occasion, one of Byrd's accusers had submitted a fabricated burglary report to the police.

Attorney Fleming now pressed the police for permission to have Byrd undergo the lie detector test he had demanded four months earlier. Permission was finally granted.

Dee Wheeler, a lie detector examiner of recognized ability, was summoned. As Wheeler prepared his subject for the test, Byrd beamed, so certain was he that he would be vindicated.

When the test was over, Wheeler told the attorney and the police that the examination disclosed that Byrd was telling nothing but the truth in denying any part in the station holdup. His findings were relayed to the district attorney who agreed that there remained no course but to dismiss the robbery charges against Byrd. This was done promptly, and Byrd was released from jail. But the case was far from over.

A proud man with a deep sense of morality and ethics, Byrd realized that the stigma of arrest and indictment still rested on his head. He demanded that the damning records be expunged not only from the Fort Worth files but also from the files of the FBI and all other law enforcement agencies that had received copies. Nothing was done, however.

In desperation, Byrd carried the issue to the newspapers. He begged them for some sort of intercession on his behalf. In the offices of the Fort Worth *Star-Telegram* he found sympathetic ears. Within days the paper related Byrd's story, and described his futile efforts to have the records expunged. Many readers were touched by the newspaper's accounts. Before long, letters and checks addressed to Byrd began pouring into the newspaper office. The people of Fort Worth were demanding remedial action. A search was undertaken for the two men who had originally identified Byrd as the robber, but they could not be found.

In newspaper interviews Byrd explained that during his imprisonment he had lost his car and furniture and had accumulated staggering debts. He estimated his total loss to be in excess of $6,000, a fortune to Byrd. Good friends, he asserted, had loaned money to his wife, and he was determined to pay back every cent of every loan.

"Some day I'll get out of this financial hole," he said, "but what worries me is that I can't get my name removed from the public records. People always want to think the worst of others, and what will they be thinking of me with a bad record on the books? Some will still believe that I'm a robber unless the record is removed.

"What kind of a life are my wife and I leading now with six thousand dollars in debts on our backs? True, I've got my old job back, but I can no longer send money to my brothers and sisters. My wife and I can't even fish any more. We lost the car. What lies ahead for us?"

People began demanding explanations from public officials, and while most of them agreed that Byrd should have been allowed to take the lie detector test at the time of his arrest, they claimed there was little that could be done.

"What about others in the same boat?" Fort Worth's citizens began asking their officials. The community of Fort Worth was up in arms, the Byrd case was on every tongue, and many a law-abiding man said to his neighbor: "This could really happen to me—to any of us."

Public officials had their say, usually in response to reporters' questions. Said Attorney General Waggoner Carr: "Texas may need a law requiring lie detector tests for accused persons who request them." He added that if Byrd had been give a test after his first request, it would have opened the eyes of everyone connected with the case.

But Carr did not advocate a law permitting victims of unwarranted arrest to sue the state for their losses of time and employment or the stigma of a police record. He stated that a person illegally or unjustly incarcerated might be entitled to compensation from someone, but he doubted the wisdom of allowing suits against the state in cases where officers have done nothing more than hold a person on complaint of a citizen. Byrd, he explained, was entitled to bring a civil suit against the person who unjustly accused him but stood little chance of recovering his losses.

Others pointed out that a file showing the Byrd case was dismissed might not satisfy a prospective employer and could cause enhancement of penalty if the subject was ever convicted on another charge in the future.

Sheriff Lon Evans was quick to say that his department's policy was to grant a lie detector test to every person requesting one. He said he agreed that passing such a test did not justify releasing a person who had been identified as the perpetrator of a crime. "However," he added "if a person did pass a test, it would make us suspicious enough of our case to check into the complainant's background. That's the principal reason we give such tests."

Texas lawmakers soon took notice of the Byrd case and its implications. Several clamored for new and protective legislation. State Senator Don Kennard and Congressman Don Gladden announced they were studying the situation with a view toward proposing possible legislative remedies that would prevent a similar situation from arising again. Kennard spoke of establishing a public defender department for Texas, and Gladden said he was studying a proposal that would require the police to provide a lie detector test when a suspect demanded it. According to Gladden, "No person should be *required* to take a lie detector test; but when a man asks for one, I don't think it is any burden on the police to give him one."

Meanwhile, newspapers continued to call for the immediate expunging of Byrd's arrest from police records. Said the Fort Worth *Star-Telegram* in an editorial:

Does the expunging of the wrongful police record of Mr. Byrd have to hinge on something that may never take place? . . . Why shouldn't the evidence on which dismissal of the indictment was based—a lie detector among other things—be sufficient for the police?

Independent investigation and the gathering of confirmatory evidence are fine—up to a point. But the matter of clearing the record of a man held to have been in no way connected with a crime should not drag on because of a possibility that may never develop.

The debate dragged on, but at this writing, long afterward, the records of Byrd's arrest and the circumstances surrounding it have disappeared from the files of the Fort Worth police. But have they vanished from the files of the FBI and other police departments around the country?

Following the Byrd case, the lie detector reached a popularity it had never before known in Texas. Soon after Byrd's release, the Fort Worth prosecutor ordered a polygraph test for a 36-year-old truck driver, McKinley Powell, who had been accused of murder months before. After Powell had passed the examination, his accuser confessed to the crime.

Only a day after Powell's release from custody, a test was ordered for Donald G. Carter, aged 19, who had spent three months in jail awaiting trial for a burglary that he insisted he had not committed. When the test showed that Carter was telling the truth, the police reopened their investigation and, to their embarrassment, belatedly discovered that Carter had been telling the truth from the beginning—he had been in state prison on another charge at the time the burglary was committed.

Fort Worth police, disturbed by these situations, promptly announced that a lie detector test would henceforth be available to any suspect requesting one. That satisfied many—but by no means all—of the citizens. Some people pointed out that the tested suspect is always at the mercy of his examiner, whose competence is the determining factor. Others cited a study which showed that a *good* polygraphist is wrong three out of ten times. How often, they wondered, did an inexperienced operator misread or misinterpret the machine's graph?

Byrd's experience aroused keen interest in the lie detector not only in Texas but throughout the United States. People who knew little or nothing about the polygraph came forward with many questions. How did it all start? Who invented the instrument? What are the underlying principles behind the technique? What can the lie detector accomplish? And what are its limitations? There were many other questions calling for answers. Some of the explanations will follow in succeeding chapters of this book.

CHAPTER

2

How It Began

In the middle of the nineteenth century Dr. Hans Gross, an Austrian known as "the father of criminalistics," defined the search for truth as the basis and goal of all criminal investigations.

"In a certain sense," he asserted, "a large part of the criminalist's work is nothing more than a battle against lies. He has to discover the truth and must fight the opposite. He meets the opposite at every step."

No doubt Dr. Gross, who died in 1915, knew that in 1895 a celebrated Italian, Cesare Lombroso, was experimenting with primitive mechanical and scientific equipment to ascertain whether suspected offenders or important witnesses were speaking the truth or lying. Lombroso based his answers on changes or lack of changes in blood pressure and heart beat of his subjects while they underwent intensive examination.

Lombroso pioneered no new methods for his technique; he merely used instruments invented years before for medical purposes. Therefore, authorities insist that in no sense was Lombroso "the inventor" of what is now popularly used and known as the lie detector or polygraph.

No doubt Gross and Lombroso were both aware of the crying need for a new and more efficient means of lie detection—some scientific technique far different from the torturous and often barbaric means of trial that had their origin in antiquity.

The histories of ancient civilizations contain records of brutal trials by ordeal. Well-known is the old Oriental custom of feeding a mouthful of rice to a person suspected of crime. The victim would be judged guilty if he could not easily and quickly spit the rice from his mouth—a test predicated on the fact that fear and tenseness usually inhibit the creation of saliva.

And there was King Solomon, who was once called upon to determine which of two women was speaking the truth in claiming a small child as her own. Ordering the child to be cut in two, the ruler reasoned that the truthful woman would willingly relinquish her claim in order to save a life and that the liar would not challenge his edict.

Another ancient method of determining truth required a suspect to grasp a white-hot metal rod and carry it to a designated point. Then the seared hand would be carefully bandaged. If the scars did not heal by a certain day, the accused would be considered guilty and punished as the codes decreed. There were many such "tests," most of them too shocking and brutal for description.

Lombroso's scientific experiments to determine whether or not a person was telling the truth attracted wide attention until he died in 1909 at the age of 73. Lombroso never realized that he had paved the way for today's general use of the lie detector not only for criminal investigations but also for domestic, industrial, and governmental conflicts.

The pioneering work of Gross and Lombroso inspired other criminologists to carry on. Many rallied to the challenge, asking themselves the same questions over and over: Can a liar be betrayed only by clever investigative work or can his own emotional and physical responses be used to trap him? Can a scientific instrument designed to test human emotions and physical changes wring the truth from a person bent on lying?

The answers would not come until many years later, after the refinement of Lombroso's lie detector. And even with these refinements and its growing use in the United States and a few foreign countries, the proper use of the polygraph continues to be a highly controversial subject.

Today the lie detector is used more often by defense counsel than by prosecutors and law enforcement officials. Its chief function is to clear the wrongly accused innocent, not to convict the guilty. However, there are notable exceptions. For example, an informant or an eyewitness, speaking the truth in a polygraph examination, may confirm a theory on which crime investigators are working or divulge valuable information leading to the offender. One recent illustration of the positive use of the polygraph occurred in San Francisco, where officers investigating an apartment house fire eliminated a number of suspected arsonists by testing them with the lie detector.

Supporters of lie detector methods insist that the technique is more than 90 percent accurate, that it is difficult for the most cunning offender to deceive an experienced polygraph operator, and that the value of the polygraph in crime detection is unquestioned. Others, however, contend that the polygraph has never been accepted by the scientific community, and many libertarians question the fairness of the lie detector, arguing that it unjustly robs a suspect of his innermost secrets. Testimony gleaned through polygraph examinations has been accepted unconditionally as legal evidence in only a few states; elsewhere the results of such tests are accepted as admissible testimony only when both sides in a specific issue have agreed in a pre-trial stipulation to accept them.

The polygraph only records changes in such physiological reactions as pulse, breathing rate, and blood pressure. From these recordings, the polygraphist proposes to accomplish that which the instrument cannot—he must reach a conclusion as to the meaning of its recordings.

In other words, he must interpret the polygraph's data.

This author leaves the question of polygraph credibility to the reader, who should know that the late J. Edgar Hoover, for many years director of the Federal Bureau of Investigation, was unimpressed by the claimed value of the polygraph; and that Richard M. Nixon, once a practicing lawyer, said, "I don't know how accurate they [lie detector findings] are, but I know they'll scare the hell out of people." He was referring, of course, to the large number of individuals who, through the years, have confessed their guilt after being confronted with the results of a lie detector test.

While the late William Howard Taft, then chief justice of the

United States Supreme Court, made no public comment on the legal status of the lie detector, he did say, "I believe, and I regret to say it, that throughout this country the administration of criminal law and the prosecution of crime are a disgrace to our civilization."

Despite disagreements among experts over the value of polygraph findings as legal evidence, there are many who believe that only time and change of approach in the use of the lie detector will overcome opposition to the method.

Early study of the polygraph method provoked the interest of Professor Hugo Munsterberg, Harvard's pioneer in criminal psychology, who spent years trying to determine the value of the oath taken by a witness or a defendant before testifying. With a dim view of the conventional promise "to tell the truth and nothing but the truth," Munsterberg wrote in 1907 that while the religious nature of the oath may eliminate an intention to hide the truth, "it fails to increase the capacity for truthful statements." A severe critic of the worth of eyewitness testi-mony, Munsterberg readily admitted that the oath may help in obtaining "objective truth."

Munsterberg's deep interest in finding scientific ways to uncover falsehoods was inspired, no doubt, by his profound distrust of eyewitness testimony. He claimed that no two people give similar descriptions of an incident they have observed. Once, to prove his point, the psychologist tried an experiment that received wide publicity. In the midst of a classroom discussion, he jumped from his desk and fired a revolver three times into the air. When he later asked his students to describe the incident, no two gave the same account. If intelligent, supposedly observant, and honest people differed in reporting what they had seen, Munsterberg reasoned, what could be expected of people of medium or low mentality, some of whom might have reason to attempt deception?

In the early 1920's a Texas obstetrician, Dr. R. E. House, introduced what he believed to be a new and accurate method for ascertaining the truth in criminal investigations. It called for the use of what came to be known as truth serum. He believed that a person questioned while under influence of the drug scopolamine would be unable to tell a lie.

Frustrated by a lack of funds to pursue his experiments, Dr. House died while in the midst of his work. Shortly before his death, he expressed confidence in his theory, saying that the day was not far distant when science would not only prevent 75 percent of all crimes but convict those who were guilty.

Meanwhile, other researchers were devoting their energies to what came to be known as the association test. The suspect was made to listen to the reading of some one hundred words prepared in advance. Many of the words were purposely unrelated to the crime, but interspersed among them were a few directly related to the offense. The subject was told to respond instantaneously to each word with the first thought to enter his mind. Theoretically, he would incriminate himself by his answer—or hesitation—when hearing a word associated with the crime. This theory was studied intensively by such experts as Munsterberg and Dr. John H. Wigmore, a widely acclaimed specialist in the field and a former president of the American Institute of Criminal Law and Criminology, but research soon turned to other directions.

Many believe that Lombroso's initial experiments in lie detection would probably not have resulted in the scientifically refined lie detector in present-day use had it not been for the work of three Californians in the early 1920's. One of them was the late Dr. John A. Larson, a onetime policeman in the college city of Berkeley on the east side of San Francisco Bay, who later became assistant state criminologist of Illinois. Sharing credits and honors with Dr. Larson were the late August Vollmer, the founder and chief of Berkeley's celebrated "scientific police department" and a former professor of criminology at the University of California; and Leonarde Keeler, a patrolman who later became a staff member of Northwestern University's Scientific Crime Detection Laboratory.

Vollmer was probably the first police chief in the country to voice unqualified support for the lie detector. He often said the polygraph provided the only safe and fair means of determining a person's veracity. Working together as a team, Vollmer, Larson, and Keeler developed the version of the lie detector currently in use. Their instrument used pens to record on a moving strip of graph paper the changes in a subject's heart beat, blood pressure, respiration, and electrical skin reaction as he underwent steady questioning. Their lie detector worked on the theory that if the subject were lying, his emotional and physical stress would cause the lines on the moving graph to rise and jerk above previously established normal levels.

Some of the team's first experiments provoked severe criticism from those who did not comprehend the technique used. These critics argued that tension and nervousness resulting from a mere realization that a vital test was under way would naturally produce false and misleading indications on the graph. However, Vollmer, Larson, and Keeler were quick and eager to dispel that misconception. They explained, as present polygraphists do, that testing always begins with a long series of deliberately innocuous questions, or control inquiries. These questions in no way involve the crime. Not until the subject has established a normal level of graphic reactions does the examiner subtly and with no change of voice or facial expression inject the "dynamite question," which pointedly and directly refers to the offense. The graphic results, when examined and interpreted by an expert, would indicate whether or not the subject was lying.

Even today, some unlicensed and inexperienced lie detector operators fail to interpret the graphs correctly or are tricked by a cunning subject, but the expert polygraphist is always alert and can keep erroneous conclusions to a minimum.

Dr. Larson is generally credited with the development of the lie detector as it is used today, but it was Keeler who later refined Larson's original equipment. Dr. Larson recorded many of his early experiments in his book, *Lying and Its Detection*, published in 1938. It relates the case of a housewife who reported the theft of a $20 bill from her home, which apparently had been entered through a jimmied window. The police, without a clue, questioned many people, including a family friend who was considered above suspicion even though he was the last person known to have left the house.

The man eventually volunteered to take a lie detector test but assured the officers that he would be quickly vindicated. The graph recorded no changes as he answered questions on unrelated matters, such as his smoking habits, his job, and his taste in movies. Then he was asked point blank: "Did you steal a twenty dollar bill?" He promptly answered, "No," but at that point the polygraph pens jumped far above the normal lines, establishing the falsity of his denial. Yet even with this evidence neither the detectives nor the family could believe him guilty.

A day later, shortly before the man was to be eliminated as a suspect, Larson proposed a second test. Again the pens disclosed deception. Advised of the results, the man finally admitted his guilt, saying, "The machine has the goods on me."

Another case related by Larson revealed how confessions obtained through a lie detector test often lead to the capture of others involved in the same crime. This case concerned a gang of eight youths from 18 to 20 years of age, who robbed couples in a lovers' lane.

Only two of the young gangsters were captured, and they stubbornly insisted they had done no wrong. However, when polygraph tests demonstrated that they were lying, they broke down, admitted their guilt, and named their six accomplices. The others were rounded up and gave full confessions, admitting to a number of other crimes of which they had not previously been suspected.

Shortly after this, Larson recalled, a storekeeper complained to the police that he could no longer endure the steady round of shoplifting going on in his place. Asked for a list of customers who might be responsible, he named thirty-eight college girls. As he mentioned one name, however, he hesitated, explaining that the young woman was the daughter of a wealthy family and would have no reason to steal.

Larson, working as usual with Chief Vollmer, decided to test all of the coeds including the rich one, and the group consented. Examination of the first seventeen by the lie detector brought only negative results. But when the eighteenth, the student from the affluent family, was questioned, sudden changes in the recordings pointed to her guilt. Faced with the results, the student confessed, admitting she was unable to resist a compulsion to steal and had pilfered hundreds of dollars worth of expensive merchandise "just for the thrill of it."

Larson and his associates always took pride in their ability to clear the innocent as well as to incriminate the guilty. To illustrate, they recounted the case of two men jailed as bank robbers. The trial had been under way for several days when counsel for the defense obtained court permission for a polygraph test.

Despite the instrument's positive indication that the defendants were telling the truth, the trial continued. Time for closing arguments was drawing near when the sheriff sent word that two men, arrested only an hour before, had confessed to the bank robbery, describing the crime in such detail that there could be no doubt of their guilt. The trial ended abruptly, and two innocent men walked out of the courtroom free.

Larson also described an extraordinary case in which one Alfred Lingle was shot to death in what was judged to be a gang murder. After long investigation, a man named Bell confessed his participation in the crime and implicated an accomplice named Sullivan. Bell's story created grave doubts, and a lie detector examination, conducted by Larson, indicated that the entire story was false. Subsequent inquiry led to the conclusion that Bell had lied deliberately to throw the blame on Sullivan because the latter had stolen Bell's sweetheart and deserted him after his arrest.

A strange situation once occurred in an eastern penitentiary when a superstitious and not-very-intelligent prisoner asked his cellmates whether it was possible to fool the lie detector. In jest, they told him that if he wore a small bottle of alcohol over his heart during the polygraph test, the machine would be unable to record changes in heart beats. The prisoner did just that, not knowing that the examiner had been forewarned. After the suspect had answered a number of simple and unrelated questions, he was finally asked: "Did you do anything to prevent this test from working?"

"No," came the quick response, but despite the bottle the graph showed a sudden and sharp rise in pulse. Further questions convinced the authorities of his guilt beyond any doubt.

Another humorous case, ingeniously solved through the efforts of Rudolph H. Capute, a brilliant and busy New York polygraphist, merits mention here largely because it supports Capute's belief in the accuracy of the lie detector.

This case involved the disappearance of well-filled money bags from the storeroom of a bank. After a vain hunt for clues, the police turned their suspicions toward an illiterate neighborhood woman, who in broken English vigorously denied any knowledge of the theft.

As the investigation continued, an officer learned that the woman's boyfriend was a butcher. The information was relayed to Capute, who had been called in to assist with the polygraph, and his quick mind suddenly grasped a new line of questioning.

Subjecting the woman to intensive lie detector examination, Capute posed question after question, all of them involving phrases using the word "meet" in its proper connotation. His theory was that an illiterate woman hearing the word so frequently spoken in its proper meaning would become confused by an image of "meat," and therefore turn her thoughts to her butcher friend and his likely involvement.

The ruse worked, and in due time both the woman and the butcher confessed their guilt, explaining they had hidden their loot in two open sides of a beef carcass and then bound the sections together with rope.

How It Works

O ne of the clearest and most nontechnical explanations of
the workings of the modern lie detector can be found in
the April 1961 issue of the *Yale Law Journal* in an article written
by Jerome H. Skolnick, then assistant professor of law and
sociology at Yale. Speaking of the polygraph, he wrote:

Perhaps the most intriguing quality is to be found in the
curious position it holds in the field of criminal procedure and
evidence. While the polygraph appears to be in wide use, its
results have been excluded from trials even when sought to be
introduced by the accused. The exclusionary policy of the
courts has, however, been attacked by some leading commentators on evidence, who favor introducing lie detector results
in civil and criminal trials, and who even suggest that there is
something unscientific about a legal system which bars such
evidence. Their eagerness to introduce the technique probably
arises out of the fact that out of all problems associated with
human testimony—accuracy of perception, ability to recall—
none can be considered more destructive to justice out of a
trial than a lying witness.

Turning to the early history of the polygraph and to
Lombroso's pioneering work Mr. Skolnick stated:

John A. Larson, perhaps the most scholarly of the Chicago-
Berkeley group who sought to advance the 'science of lie

detection,' built an instrument in 1921 which he called a 'polygraph'; it combined all three measures—blood pressure, pulse, and respiration. His junior collaborator, Leonarde Keeler, added galvanic skin response to the list. Galvanic skin response is obtained by fastening electrodes to the fingertips. The fingertips are believed to show evidence of perspiration when a person is under emotional stress or is speaking falsely.

After a preliminary interview the subject is seated in a chair especially constructed to permit the attachment of the various measuring devices; the pneumograph tube is tied to his chest, the blood pressure cuff is wrapped around his upper arm, and a net of electrodes is attached to his hands. The subject looks straight ahead. The examiner is seated to his side behind a desk containing a set of controls which the subject cannot see. These instruments begin a continuous graphic recording when the examination commences.

The questions asked are based upon the results of the preliminary interview, together with available facts and circumstances forming the basis of the accusation. They also vary according to the type of person being questioned.

This explanation and those of other polygraphists induced this writer, after diligent research, to personally undergo a lie detector test. The test was given to me through the courtesy of Stephen J. Long, vice-president of the Merit Protective Service, in his San Francisco office.

Before me on a table sat the lie detector, an instrument known by its trade name, a Stuelting. The instrument itself was encased in white metal and was about the size of a small suitcase and easily portable. It was approximately twenty inches long, twelve inches wide and five inches deep. Its top surface was covered with mysterious looking knobs and little bottled ink-wells to serve the four stylus-like pens on the tips of thin, hollow metal tubes that looked like wires. I was told that two of the pens were to record respiration, the third was for pulse reaction, and the fourth was to measure galvanic skin response. These physical factors would be recorded by the pens as they moved over a wide sheet of closely lined graph paper extending from one side of the instrument. The paper, I was told, would move forward at the rate of six inches per minute.

I was instructed to sit in a chair close to the instrument so that

I could be prepared for the test. Two lengths of what is known as pneumo tubing, resembling rubber hosing, were fastened around my waist, one over the abdomen, the other some inches above. I was then instructed to raise the left sleeve of my shirt, my coat having first been removed.

Over my upper arm Mr. Long wound a cuff similar to the type a physician uses to measure blood pressure. I asked why the left arm was selected and was informed that it was nearest to the large brachial artery, an excellent artery for recording blood pressure. Small steel rings were placed over my fingertips to measure galvanic skin response. A slight flow of electricity through these electrodes would produce perspiration in response to emotional stress. In other words, my reactions to the questions would be measured in four ways—blood pressure, respiration, pulse, and galvanic skin response.

Now we were ready to start the examination, but first I tried to analyze my own thoughts and reactions as I stared blankly at this strange contraption of steel, knobs, and wires which could distinguish truth from lies. Here lay an inanimate metal device capable of probing my innermost secrets, or drawing from my well-guarded brain facts that I regarded as my own personal belongings, and of determining with apparent superhuman power whether I was an honest man or a plain liar.

It was an uncanny feeling, one I had never before experienced, and as I awaited what would follow I wondered what fears and emotions would be felt by someone for whom such a test might determine life or liberty.

Stephen Long put me somewhat at ease with a few simple questions, and as I responded truthfully I watched the pens (something the actual subjects are not permitted to do) move in almost straight, unchanged horizontal lines, the length and closeness of which could easily be measured on the paper graph.

What was my name? Where was I born? What was my occupation? Did I enjoy my work? Soon I surmised that he was now ready to spring some key questions.

"Have you verified every statement in your new book?" he suddenly inquired.

"Yes, wherever possible," I replied truthfully. The pen movements remained unchanged.

"Do you think your book will sell well?"

This time I really wanted to see how the pens would record a lie.

"Yes," I answered with a deliberate falsehood. "My publishers have guaranteed in writing that they will make my book a best seller after its first month of publication."

The pens jerked, moving wildly and with greater space between the lines. Now I knew what this meant, and so did Long.

"That was a lie, wasn't it?" he demanded with a twinkle in his eye.

I shook my head and brazenly denied having spoken falsely.

Again the pens jiggled erratically. I was trapped—branded as a liar.

Intrigued, I asked how one could become a polygraphist, what type of background was needed, and how long a student would be obliged to study.

I was told it would require a college background but not necessarily a degree. It would also involve fully six weeks of intensive work and study, costing between $1,400 and $1,600. On completion of the course, a student wishing to practice would be obliged to send his instructor a minimum of thirty-five sheets of used graph paper to indicate that he had carried out that number of tests. To practice professionally, an accepted polygraphist must be free of a police record. With this information the session ended. I knew more about the polygraph and its workings. But the fact remained—I had flunked.

4

Precedent and Breakthrough

For many years the case of *Frye v. United States* has been referred to in legal circles as a landmark and precedent in the long struggle for acceptance of lie detector evidence and testimony in courtroom proceedings. There has rarely been a court decision concerning the admissibility of polygraph examinations that failed to refer to Frye; nor do writers of dissertations on lie detection overlook the old ruling denying the validity of this technique.

This landmark case dates back to 1920, when Dr. Robert W. Brown, an affluent physician of Washington, D.C., was shot and killed in his office. A reward of $1,000 for capture and conviction of the killer spurred police to intensive action.

Close to a year had passed when officers routinely investigating a robbery case arrested a young black, James Alphonse Frye. Frye denied his guilt. When he was asked about the murder of Dr. Brown Frye stoutly insisted he was innocent of that crime and knew nothing about it.

Under further questioning, however, he finally confessed that he had shot and killed the doctor, relating details that coincided with all the facts authorities knew about the crime. His indictment followed, and he was held without bail.

Frye had trouble finding counsel, but two young lawyers seeking experience finally agreed to take his case. Much to their amazement, Frye suddenly and unexpectedly repudiated his confession. He insisted on his innocence, declaring he had confessed only because he had been offered half of the reward if he was convicted.

Although Frye told his lawyers he could provide an alibi, no witnesses could be found to support his claim. Facing a dilemma, the young attorneys turned to Dr. William M. Marston, the noted polygraphist, and asked him to subject their client to a lie detector test. Marston agreed to do so without fee.

Somewhat to Marston's surprise, the examination showed Frye to be telling the truth in denying his guilt. The trial followed, but no witnesses could be found to support any detail of Frye's story. In desperation, defense counsel offered to present Dr. Marston as their star witness, hoping his findings would be the turning point in the case. But Judge McCoy, the trial jurist and chief justice of the District of Columbia Supreme Court, took an opposite view.

The defense lawyers offered to subject the defendant to still another test, this time in open court, but Judge McCoy merely asserted: "It is too late." Mention of Marston's report and its results did, however, move the jury to spare Frye's life. The charge against him was reduced to second degree murder, and after conviction he was sentenced to life imprisonment.

From the penitentiary he continued to plead his innocence; and his lawyers appealed to the Federal Appellate court, which favored the prosecution. It ruled that Dr. Marston's test, based largely on blood pressure, lacked reliability and validity. The decision held that lie detection was still in a "twilight zone" and unworthy of recognition in a court. Frye seemed doomed to finish his life behind bars. For the next three years he continued to plead for justice. Then, unexpectedly, came the turning point. Another man confessed to the murder of Dr. Brown. At first, the authorities doubted his story, but a close investigation of every detail of the confession showed he was telling the truth. A miscarriage of justice was recognized, and the penitentiary gates opened for Frye. His freedom, however, failed to erase the high court's decision from the records, and it has survived as a precedent to this day. Many court decisions have invoked the high court's ruling as to the unreliability of the lie detector, and many an accused person has been denied an opportunity to introduce favorable polygraph findings.

For many years lawyers have pondered the Frye decision, wondering why this case assumed landmark proportions. They have several answers. One is that the issue was decided by a federal rather than a state court; the other is that the ruling came soon after the introduction of the polygraph and asserted in positive, unqualified terms that the lie detector was too unreliable to deserve court recognition. Since that time there have been other federal court decisions involving lie detector evidence, but almost all of those have ruled against its admissibility.

There is no federal statute on the subject of lie detectors. However, a procedure has evolved wherein both sides in a legal controversy and the trial judge make an agreement (called a stipulation) permitting the defendant to undergo a lie detector test with a proviso that the results, whether favorable or unfavorable to the defendant, may be used as legal evidence. If the stipulation is made before the case comes to trial, the presiding judge need not give his consent.

The stipulation procedure evolved as a compromise between contending forces in criminal cases in which one side demanded the right to a lie detector case and the other vigorously opposed such a move. Most legal authorities agree that the stipulation procedure is recognized and accepted in every state of the union. Only in California has lie detector testimony been accepted without stipulation—and then only once—in the Cutler case described later in this chapter.

One cogent illustration of the impact of the Frye decision is the case of Robert Michael Wilson in 1970, half a century after the Frye decision. Wilson, indicted in Baltimore on technical charges of violating an interstate commerce statute, moved for permission to undergo a lie detector examination at government expense. The issue came before the U.S. District Court for the District of Maryland, which ruled against Wilson in a lengthy judgment, citing numerous cases including that of Frye.

In its opinion, the court stated it had:

.... heard testimony of two days relating to the threshold issue of whether the state of the art [of lie detection] is sufficiently advanced to hold such evidence admissible.... Since polygraphy comprehends physiological and psychological theory, the evaluation of the state of the art must necessarily broaden to include any research on the theoretical aspects of the technique. Equally valuable is the knowledge and research of experienced practitioners in polygraphy, regardless of a lack of training in the underlying conceptual disciplines. Thus, rather than putting the issue in terms of 'general acceptance within a particular field' and engaging in an academic dispute as to the particular field in which polygraphy fits, the Court chooses to assess the progress of polygraphy by drawing on contributions from those engaged both in theory and practice. See *Frye v. United States.* ...

It is undisputed that the technique of polygraphy has progressed dramatically since the ruling of inadmissibility in Frye, supra. The voluminous record reflects the improvement in the machines, the gains in knowledge, and the widespread use by law enforcement and business communities.

Then followed a detailed analysis of the various components of lie detection technique:

The theory is that conscious deception causes an acute reaction in the sympathetic nervous system, translated chemically into higher rates of pulse, blood pressure, breathing, and skin resistance.... A fair statement is that while studies conducted by private and governmental organizations assess the validity and reliability of the technique at 70 to 95 percent, the systematic research relating to the validity of polygraphy is still in its formative period and is ongoing.

A study of the theory and process of the polygraph examination reveals complexities not present in the fields of fingerprint, handwriting, voiceprint, ballistics, and neutron activation analysis, all of which are based on the identity or behavior of physical phenomena. The experts and studies differ as to the capability of the polygraph industry to cope with these complexities, but none would dispute their existence. The distinction is that polygraphy, albeit based on a scientific theory, remains an art with unusual responsibility placed on the examiner. The acquainting of the examiner with the subject matter is often a source of improper suggestion conscious or subconscious. The preparation of the test and discussion with the examinee of the polygraph procedure furnishes additional opportunity for improper evaluation. The experts are in accord that the examiner must carefully watch for signs of psychosis, extreme neurosis, psychopathology, drunkenness and drugs, any of which might preclude a successful examination.

Continuing with a recital of purported weakness in the polygraph technique, the decision concluded:

Accordingly, it is this sixth day of July, 1973, by the United States District Court of Maryland, ordered that the motion to permit the testimony of polygraph witnesses filed on behalf of defendant Wilson be not granted and the same is hereby denied.

A breakthrough in California occurred in November 1972 in the case of Raymond Christopher Cutler. It involved some statements purportedly made by Cutler in a controversial encounter with a deputy U.S. marshal in the Los Angeles International Airport

Highly significant is the November 9, 1972 ruling of Superior Court Judge Allan Miller that scientific tests have shown lie detector equipment and technique to be so accurate that rules against them in courtrooms should be changed.

Cutler's arrest took place in the airport on August 25, 1971, when the deputy marshal became suspicious of a suitcase which Cutler was carrying. Cutler was asked to open it for inspection, and his reply sparked the controversy between him and the officer.

Cutler later contended that he refused such permission; but the deputy marshal swore that he had been told to open the luggage—which, according to the arresting officer, was found to contain marijuana. While Cutler was formally charged with illegal possession of marijuana, his attorney, Barry Tarlow, chose to base his defense on the claim that the suitcase had been opened in defiance of the accused man's refusal and that the search was therefore illegal.

Both men in the controversy willingly subjected themselves to lie detector tests with the court's approval. No stipulation was required. The examiner, a specialist of acknowledged experience and ability, reported that Cutler's declaration that he had definitely refused permission to open and search the luggage was a truthful statement. It was this issue, and not the question of marijuana possession, that brought the case before Judge Miller.

The judge's decision, rendered after long consideration, was exhaustive. After citing the Frye ruling, he moved into an analysis of the qualifications of polygraphists, pointing out that they must always guard against their subjects' efforts to deceive them. He then asserted that the polygraph has a high degree of accuracy, from 78 to 90 percent, and that its major purpose was the search for truth. He was careful to note that the advancement of polygraphy as a science had far increased its accuracy until it now enjoyed general acceptance. He also noted that the federal government uses this technique, accepting it as reliable.

The judge further stated that although most courts, local and federal, will not accept the results of lie detector tests, the courts are greatly in need of some way to determine the truthfulness of defendants and witnesses. The final judgment of a jurist, he noted, may depend on the credibility of the accused, explaining:

> Perjury is prevalent, and the oath taken by witnesses has little effect to deter false testimony. The principal role of the trier of fact is the search for truth, and any reasonable procedure or method to assist the court in this search should be employed.

Thus, the court accepted the results of Cutler's lie detector test and based its ruling on that test. Judge Miller's significant decision was followed by the district attorney's notice of intention to file an appeal. After more than a year had passed without such action being taken, the request was finally withdrawn, a move the defense contended was prompted by a realization that such an appeal would fail. The impact of Judge Miller's decision on future cases remains to be seen.

It is important to note that in the lapse of forty-nine years between the Frye decision in 1920 and the Cutler ruling in 1972, there was only one other breakthrough in the acceptance of polygraph testimony. This occurred in 1938 in New York in the celebrated case of Raymond Kenny (see in Chapter 13).

Not long after Judge Miller's decision, a bill contrary to its spirit was signed by Governor Edmund Gerald Brown, Jr., of California. It spelled out broad new rights for police officers under investigation for alleged wrongdoing. Popularly known as the police officers' bill of rights, the measure permits law enforcement officers to refuse to take a lie detector test. It further provides that such a refusal cannot be held against the officer. Still another provision states that photographs and addresses of officers under investigation cannot be released without consent of the person involved. In addition, officers "under interrogation shall not be subjected to visits by the press or news media without expressed consent."

During legislative debates on the measure before its passage, opponents contended it would unfairly give police officers more privileges than other citizens, and that a lie detector sometimes provides the only means for uncovering official wrongdoing.

5

Tests by Stipulation

Throughout legal history it has been shown that defendants do not always benefit by availing themselves of polygraph tests under stipulation. Too often a defendant tries to fool the lie detector and vindicate himself despite strong circumstantial and direct evidence against him. Such a case is that of William Jack Houser of California. Lawyers agree the case is one of the first on record in which a stipulation was allowed, and for that reason it is often referred to in high court decisions.

William Houser was arrested in Tulare County on July 4, 1947, on three charges resulting from the complaint of 8-year-old Patsy Ann Jeter, an unusually alert third-grade student. On the basis of her complaint, Houser faced three charges—lewd and lascivious conduct toward the child, rape by force, and statutory rape.

Houser was brought to trial before Judge Glenn L. Moran. When the trial opened, a motion for dismissal of the last two charges was granted and Houser was obliged to face a jury on the count involving lewd conduct.

Little Patsy Ann's story was a shocking account of sexual mistreatment. Promising to tell only the truth, and acknowledging that she knew what it meant to tell a lie, she said that on the night of July 4 she had been left in her mother's parked car with her little sister, aged 3, on a street in front of the Lindsay Club, where her father was then playing cards in the back room. Her mother, Patsy said, had gone in to ask him to accompany them home. Patsy said her mother had returned to the car several times to make certain she and her sister were safe. Patsy related that at about 11 o'clock a strange man had approached the car and asked her if she would like a pound box of candy.

Unable to resist such an offer, Patsy said she left the car, barefooted, and accompanied the man down the street. He told her that the candy was in a nearby orange grove. Patsy and the stranger had walked some distance when he suddenly turned against her, tore off her panties and her dress, and violated her sexually despite her protests.

Patsy said that after the man abandoned her in the orchard, she ran terrified to the place where the car had been parked. Finding it gone, she decided to wait for her parents to return. Meanwhile, her mother and father, frightened by her absence, had driven to their home a short distance away, intending to return to the parking place if they did not find their daughter.

When they finally did return to the parking place, little Patsy, clad only in her underclothes, ran into their outstretched arms. As soon as she had related all the details of her experience, the police were notified.

"Can you tell me, Patsy, what the man looked like?" an officer had asked. "Tell me everything; it'll help us to capture him."

Patsy had retained a vivid mental picture of her assailant. "His hair was a sort of a brownish-black," she related. "He had a pointed nose. His sleeves were rolled up—and he smelled of whisky."

"His clothes—can't you remember what he was wearing?" she was asked.

"Oh, yes," she quickly recalled. "He wore a sort of a khaki-colored shirt. His pants looked bluish, and I noticed that he wore a belt."

The child was then taken to the office of a physican who confirmed that she had been sexually violated. Search for the assailant then began in earnest.

Patsy led the officers to the orange orchard and pointed to the exact spot where she claimed the assault had taken place. Carefully following the path, the policemen observed her barefoot tracks and the shoe marks presumably made by her assailant. Identification experts were sent for at once to make plaster of paris casts of the impressions in the soft dirt.

As the hunt continued, officers picked up two suspects. Patsy looked at them and shook her head. "Not them," she said positively. A third suspect, William Jack Houser, was arrested on suspicion. Patsy said she was not certain he was the guilty one, adding that he "looked like" the culprit but that she could not be positive.

"Is this the man?" the district attorny demanded sharply as suspect and child faced each other. "I can't be sure," was her frank reply. "I really don't know."

At a police line-up the following morning, Patsy looked at Houser standing with a group of six prisoners and she readily pointed to him, stating that now she was positive of her identification. Houser was then asked to explain his movements on the crucial night of July 4. He responded that he had been drinking heavily all of that day but was not really intoxicated. He said he had made the rounds of local bars in the evening and that after nightfall he had been in the Lindsay Bar watching the poker table until shortly before 11 o'clock, at which time he'd walked out of the rear door and gone home alone.

After detailing the block-to-block route he said he had followed, the police accompanied him to his home, where he lived with his elderly father and 8-year-old sister.

"Let's see the clothes you wore last night," one of the officers requested. Houser explained that he had washed them early that morning and that they were on the line with other garments he had washed at the same time. When the police asked to see the shoes he wore, Houser pointed to his newly cleaned shoes, which he said had been shined that morning.

Leaving Houser at his home, the officers returned to the orange grove, where they measured the footprints for size. The plaster casts together with Houser's shoes, samples of soil, and Patsy's dress were sent to the State Bureau of Identification in Sacramento for laboratory examination.

The dress was scrutinized by Officer Bradford, one of the technicians, who announced that it was impossible to identify blood groups from the clothing because it was smeared with dirt, but he did conclude without qualification that Houser's shoes perfectly matched the plaster casts. To verify that opinion he pointed out that the trademark "Regent" was visible on both shoe and cast. In fact, he called attention to exactly eight points of similarity between the two. "I'd say," he reported, "that there's barely one chance in a hundred thousand that the print and the cast were not made by the same shoe," a conclusion regarded by the police as highly significant.

By this time, detectives were reasonably certain of Houser's guilt, but to further verify their judgment they turned to the lie detector. It was at this point that the legal agreement or stipulation concerning test results was made. According to the legal requirements of such agreements, both the defense counsel and the prosecutor agreed in writing that the results of the examination, favorable or unfavorable, could be used in court by either side.

A trained officer, Albert Riedel from the Berkeley Police Department, was summoned to administer the test. On completion of the polygraph, he reported his certainty that Houser had not given truthful answers to all questions. Riedel was later called upon to testify at Houser's trial. His statements were decidedly harmful to the defense. They corroborated Officer Bradford's recital of his work with the shoes and footprint casts.

While on the stand, Riedel exhibited the lie detector equipment and the test graphs, explaining their purpose and the mechanical workings of the instrument. He said that he had asked the defendant ten questions, each calling for a "yes" or "no" answer, alternating the inquiries so that half related to the crime and half had no bearing on the case. He told judge and jury that, in his opinion, Houser's responses to those questions pertaining directly to the offense were untruthful.

The defendant, seated with his lawyer, winced as he listened to this testimony. With full confidence of vindication by the polygraph, he had willingly signed the stipulation which allowed the polygraph results to be admitted as testimony. "Guess I cooked my own goose," he whispered to his attorney.

The jurors asked no questions, but it was apparent that they had been deeply impressed by the testimony and the expert's conclusions. After the state had rested its case, Houser took the witness stand. He told of his Army record and his honorable discharge, asserting that after returning to civilian life he had worked steadily to support his father and sister.

Asked in cross-examination to detail his movements on the day of the assault, he related a long and somewhat rambling story. He admitted he had been drinking so heavily that he could not recall how long he had remained home after returning there at about 7:30 P.M. He did tell of a visit to the Lindsay Club where he evidently "blacked out" and started for home with no idea of time. He claimed to have arisen at 7:30 the next morning and done the family washing. His chores completed, he had returned to town where he had been stopped by an officer and taken to Patsy's home for identification. As to the crime itself, he swore that he could not remember committing it but that he did believe "he would not do such a thing."

A number of character witnesses followed him to the stand. All testified that they knew him to be a man of truth, honesty, integrity, and morality.

On cross-examination the prosecutor delved deeply into Houser's past with a number of embarrassing questions to the character witnesses. It was the state attorney's hope that one of them would know that Houser had once pleaded guilty to public intoxication and on one occasion had been suspected of committing sodomy on a boy of ten.

A few admitted hearing such reports, but Houser, taking the stand again, tried to minimize the seriousness of such previous difficulties. The state, however, introduced documentary evidence to support the accused man's problems with the law. There was a flurry in the courtroom when it was revealed that one of the defendant's character witnesses had been convicted of statutory rape.

Defense counsel now launched an attack on the prosecution's earlier technical evidence. The jury was shown a plaster cast of the orchard footprint along with the defendant's shoe, and Houser's lawyer attempted to show that they were different in appearance. The effort apparently was unimpressive.

In the end, it took the jury little time to find Houser guilty of lewd conduct. A motion for a new trial having been denied, defense counsel immediately appealed on a number of grounds, some technical, others based on the claim of insufficient evidence to convict.

Among other contentions, the motion for a new trial stated that Patsy's identification of Houser was "unworthy of credence" and should have been rejected and that the identification of the shoe and its imprint was "shot with inconsistencies." The lie detector test came under strong attack, with the defense arguing that testimony in this regard was erroneously admitted as evidence. The lie detector stipulation, even though it had been agreed to and signed by the defendant, was claimed to have been improper and prejudicial to the defendant's rights. The expertise of the operator was also challenged.

Various other charges of prejudicial error and misconduct were made against the prosecutor, who was accused of having asked improper questions, one of which implied that Houser suffered from syphilis. Finally, his closing argument to the jury was attacked. In fact, no element of the state's case was overlooked in the long list of objections and charges of error listed by the defense.

Houser waited impatiently to learn his fate. The decision of the Appellate Court did not come until May 26, 1948, and it contradicted nearly every objection raised in the convicted man's behalf. The girl's identification of the accused was said to be proper evidence, and the lie detector testimony was upheld without question in view of the earlier stipulation between defense and prosecution. The high court had much to say in upholding the use of lie detector evidence, especially under the stipulation conditions in which it was presented.

Disputing the defense contentions on this phase of the trial, the justices said:

It is claimed that such evidence has no evidentiary value and that such class of evidence is not regarded by the courts and therefore it was improperly admitted.

It appears from the written stipulation signed by defendant and his counsel that the operator thereof, Mr. Riedel, is an expert in interpreting results of such tests. It was stipulated that such evidence, i.e., the questions propounded by said operator and the answers given by said defendant and the recordings of said defendant's reactions thereto, and everything appertaining to said test and the results of said test, including the opinions of said operator, be received in evidence either on behalf of the people or on behalf of the defendant ... and that said defendant hereby waives his constitutional privilege against self-incrimination to the extent that the same may be involved in the presentation in evidence of the foregoing matters.

It would be difficult to hold that the defendant should be permitted on this appeal to take advantage of any claim that such operator was not an expert and that as to the results of the test such evidence was inadmissible, merely because it happened to indicate that he was not telling the truth when he denied to the officers that he took the girl to the orange orchard and committed the acts upon her.

In conclusion, the high court denied the appeal, holding that the stipulation was valid and that the results of the test were acceptable legal evidence. Houser's eagerness for a lie detector test had been his undoing.

In another stipulation trial many years later in Florida, the court decided a unique point. Specifically, the case involved this unprecedented question: If the polygraph expert selected by both sides in a stipulation changes his mind about the defendant's veracity, does that alter the final decision of the appeals court?

In this case, titled the *State of Florida v. Sampson Davis*, the Appellate Court gave a definite answer in which the issue of public faith was an important consideration. In 1966, nineteen years after the historic Houser case, defendant Davis pleaded not guilty to a murder charge. Davis agreed to a stipulation between his attorneys, Smith, Sheldon, and Smith of Orlando, and the prosecutor, Assistant District Attorney George Vega, Jr. The stipulation later came to be called an immunity stipulation.

Both sides agreed in writing that Davis would undergo a lie detector test administered by an expert selected by mutual agreement. It was also agreed that Davis would plead guilty to a reduced charge of manslaughter if the results of the examination were in his favor, and in this event the state stood ready to dismiss all accusations. On the other hand, if the polygraph test showed him to be lying, Davis would still plead guilty to the reduced charge but take the consequences.

Deputy Sheriff Gill was selected to conduct the examination. Proceeding with his assignment, Gill gave Davis a polygraph test and concluded that the subject had truthfully answered all questions.

Accordingly, Davis' counsel appeared before the court with a motion to quash the indictment against his client, who had properly entered a plea of guilty to the manslaughter charge.

Judge Harold S. Smith, presiding over the Circuit Court for Collier County, granted the motion, and Davis considered himself a free man. But neither he nor his lawyers anticipated the state's next move.

An appeal was filed by the prosecutor in Florida's District Court of Appeal, claiming that polygraphist Gill had changed his mind and now believed that Davis had been untruthful. The state, which originally had agreed to have Gill conduct the lie detector test, had turned to a second examiner, Cliff Powell, who had reached a different conclusion, contending that Davis' answers to questions showed evidence of deception. His judgment was based on serious criticism of Gill's technique.

Advised of Powell's conclusion, Gill changed his mind, explaining that his unexpected reversal of judgment was motivated not by Powell's adverse opinion but by Powell's disapproval of Gill's techniques. Powell had emphasized that the result of any polygraph test depended on the operator.

Gill's new position thus became a major issue in the appeal. Defense counsel contended that since the selection of Gill had met with the agreement of both sides, it was for the court to rely on his original judgment—as it had by quashing the indictment. The immunity stipulation also came in for attack. Faced with this unusual problem, the Appellate Court justices labored long and hard before finally reaching a decision in Davis' favor. The high court affirmed the ruling of the trial court in dismissing the charges against the accused.

The Appellate Court decision first confirmed the legality of the stipulation, which the state had questioned, with these words:

Promises of immunity from prosecution made to a witness by a prosecuting officer with the consent of the court are justified on the ground of public policy. ... The courts treat such promises as pledges of the public faith. ... The promise alleged in the instant plea [that of the prosecuting attorney with the approval of the court] is equally a pledge of the public faith which in our opinion should be duly kept.

Concluding with an opinion on the issue between Gill and Powell, the high court expressed itself as follows:

The state's final contention is that the results of the examination were 'inconclusive' and thus, according to the agreement, neither party was bound. The state relies upon Cliff Powell's testimony for this proposition, but we cannot agree. The agreement was that the polygraph test would be given by a person selected by the parties. Deputy Gill was that person.

His conclusion was that defendant was telling the truth. Gill admitted that his later change of 'opinion' was really Powell's. Powell admitted that his opinion was not based upon any re-examination of the defendant but upon his disapproval of one of Gill's techniques and that the outcome of a polygraph examination depended largely upon the operator. Deputy Gill, not Powell, was the agreed upon operator and his opinion before it was 'changed' by Powell should control.

For the foregoing reasons, the ruling of the trial court is affirmed.

That courts intend to follow the original precedent set on the accepted stipulated lie detector tests became manifest in a decision rendered as recently as November 18, 1975. The decision came from the North Carolina Court of Appeals in the case of Dallas Steele, convicted of writing and cashing a forged money order.

Steele's accuser was Wilbur T. Foushee, owner of several stores known as Foushee's Jiffy Markets. He had complained that on the night of October 14, 1975, his store in Charlotte was broken into and robbed of twenty-eight blank money orders.

Nine days later Teresa Green, a teller in a Charlotte bank, questioned a money order which a man, later identified as Steele, presented to be cashed. She called bank headquarters, reported the number of the check involved, and learned that it had been stolen. Presumably it was one of those taken by the burglar.

Because the money order bore Steele's signature he was arrested. In court, handwriting expert Lawrence A. Kelly testified that the signature was that of Steele. But Steele insisted on his innocence.

Opposing counsel then entered into a stipulation for a lie detector test to which Steele agreed. The examination was given by Officer W. L. Holmberg, a polygraph expert for the Charlotte Police Department. He subsequently testified, by virtue of the stipulation, that some of Steele's responses showed deception.

Steele later took the stand and swore he had not known that the money order had been stolen. Nevertheless, he was found guilty and sentenced to serve not less than eight months in the state's prison or more than ten years under supervision of the Department of Correction. He appealed immediately, contending that the admission of the polygraph test results was illegal and prejudicial despite the stipulation.

In deciding the appeal, the North Carolina high court ruled against Steele, upholding the validity of the stipulation and citing rulings in the Houser and Frye cases. Said the Appellate Court:

> While the weight of authority repudiates the polygraph as an instrument of evidence in the trial of criminal cases, a few courts have recognized an exception to the general exclusionary rule. This exception arises when the parties have stipulated before the trial that test results should be admissible on behalf of either the prosecution or defense. Courts which have considered the effect of a stipulation have not been consistent as to a result.

Steele is now serving time at Central Prison in Raleigh, North Carolina.

Who's Who in Polygraphy

If one were to ask an authority to name the most prominent polygraphists in practice today, the answer would undoubtedly be: "John Reid of Chicago, Warren Holmes of Miami, and Cleve Backster and Rudolph R. Caputo, both of New York." The authority would be likely to add flattering words for several deceased polygraphists, men who have left well-earned marks of distinction in their field. Among them are Dr. John A. Larson of Berkeley, California, recognized as the inventor of the original lie detector, and Leonarde Keeler of Chicago, who developed Larson's first mechanism into an advanced instrument that still bears his name.

Actually there are hundreds if not thousands of men and women polygraphists throughout the country. They work on private cases and as technicians for law enforcement agencies. Most of them, operating institutes of their own, command large fees.

John Reid, a graduate of Chicago's DePaul University Law School, is said to have accepted the first job offered him, with the Chicago police department, where he learned to operate Keeler's equipment. Before long, he was persuaded to resign from the police force to accept a position working with Keeler on the staff of Northwestern University.

Those who have followed Reid's work recall how he once

settled a bitter controversy between two businessmen, Baker and Wetzel, who had appeared before Chicago's Municipal Judge Jacob M. Braude. Baker complained that Wetzel had never paid him for furniture valued at $1,000; Wetzel claimed that the account had been settled. Each man insisted he was telling the truth.

Judge Braude eyed the two contestants standing before him. "There's a machine called a lie detector," he told them, "that will readily tell us who is speaking the truth. A jury probably wouldn't know." He explained that the findings of lie detectors were not accepted in court as legal evidence but that in this case they might settle the issue and save everyone the expense of a trial. He stated that the cost of the test would be $15 and suggested that the loser should pay the fee. Both men agreed.

Wetzel was the first to be tested. He was given a list of questions and told to give truthful yes or no answers, which he did without deceit. The same course was followed with Baker, who eventually provided the answers that Reid had been seeking. It was Baker who brought the test to a sudden stop. "Get me out of here," he screamed. "Maybe I made a mistake. Maybe he did pay me. Perhaps I've forgotten about it."

After both men had departed, the polygraphist telephoned Judge Braude and told him that Baker had withdrawn his claim. The judge was greatly impressed with the outcome. A staunch believer in the worth of the lie detector, he predicted that someday it would be effectively used in civil and criminal cases to convict the guilty and vindicate the innocent. Braude's court records support his confidence.

There is, for example, the case of John Berg, proprietor of a small radio repair shop, who accused Henry Smith, aged 19, of stealing two electric drills from a workroom in his basement. Smith, Berg claimed, possessed the only key to the cellar.

The two contestants agreed to a lie detector test, the results of which were inconclusive, both men denying any knowledge of the theft. However, when Berg declared that no other person had used the workshop, Reid's instrument showed that the statement was false. Smith's answers to the same inquiry also showed untruthfulness. Reid then asked Smith to look at the graph recording, and the subject burst into tears. He stated that Berg had rented the basement room to a bookmaker, a fact that he hadn't wanted to disclose. Hearing this, Berg readily admitted that the back room from which the theft had occurred actually was a gambling place and that its patrons had access to Berg's office. The lie detector had settled the controversy.

Warren Holmes, now in middle age, is the former president of the Academy for Scientific Interrogation. Although he has worked on many important cases involving murders and political corruption, he is best known for his prolonged efforts to win freedom for Freddie Lee Pitts and Wilbert Lee, Florida blacks sentenced to the electric chair for the murder of two gas station employees, a crime to which another person later confessed.

Cleve Backster, who once worked for the CIA, is a strong believer in reincarnation and is deeply interested in psychic research. He is also reported to believe that plants have feelings, a theory he is said to have tested by applying polygraph electrodes to various plants to observe their peculiar "shock" reactions.

Rudolph Caputo, a genial young man, serves a large clientele in New York City. His interesting career began as director of investigations for the security firm of Smith & Wesson. His skill as a polygraphist is apparently inherited, for his father was a lie detector examiner in the Navy and later in the federal narcotics service.

A native of Brooklyn, Rudolph Caputo majored in psychology at St. John's, then studied under Backster in New York. Through the years, Caputo has played a conspicuous part in many celebrated cases, such as the controversy in which Mayor Rizzo of Philadelphia became an outstanding figure. The mayor, accused of influence peddling by Democratic Committee Chairman Peter J. Camlel, denied the charges and volunteered to subject himself to a lie detector test if his accuser would do likewise. Voicing his confidence in the polygraph, Mayor Rizzo said, "If it says a man lied, he lied." Caputo was called on to test both men. Camlel passed, but Mayor Rizzo failed, a bitter disappointment which he met with charges that the equipment was inaccurate.

The people of Philadelphia took a different view, however, for soon afterward, candidates supported by Mayor Rizzo were defeated.

Another of Caputo's best-known cases came during the Watergate investigation after Jeb Stuart Magruder testified that Attorney General John Mitchell had authorized the Watergate break-in. Called on to answer the accusation before a Senate Committee, Mitchell characterized the charge as "a palpable, damned lie." Subsequently, it was learned that Magruder had passed a lie detector test. Whether Mitchell had undergone a similar test has never been learned.

Caputo insists that the polygraph is no more subject to error than a medical diagnostic instrument. "Lie detection is not a machine but a system which uses the polygraph," he asserts. "In the hands of a competent, properly trained examiner, it is very difficult to beat. Conversely, it is very rare when it accuses someone falsely of lying. In a typical case in my own work—say the theft of negotiable bonds from a brokerage firm—I will come up with an answer about eight out of ten times, and in half of those eight cases I'll have a confession. That doesn't mean that two out of ten times somebody beats the polygraph. Usually it means that the theft was an 'outside job' and that none of the people I tested had anything to do with it."

Leonarde Keeler could have boasted of many successes. Once he tested five eyewitnesses, all respectable businessmen of Black Creek, Michigan, who had identified two men as bank robbers. The trial was under way when Keeler was summoned. His verdict—both defendants were being tried for a crime they had not committed. This conclusion was supported a day later when two men, jailed in another town for another offense, confessed to the bank robbery. The eyewitnesses said that they seriously regretted their mistake, and two innocent men were saved from the penitentiary.

This experience served to support an earlier study in which Keeler had tested some five hundred prisoners at Joliet Penitentiary, most of whom claimed to be innocent. In each case, their replies under the lie detector proved to be untruthful.

Like many other supporters of polygraph tests, Keeler believed that his technique was more reliable than the testimony of eyewitnesses. His associates agree, pointing to the case of Joseph Blazenzitz, who served sixteen years in Marquette Prison before being vindicated by the lie detector.

Blazenzitz, sentenced to life imprisonment, had nearly given up hope of release when the unexpected news arrived. It came in the form of an encouraging letter from two women who had become interested in his hobby, breeding canaries. Blazenzitz had written an article on the subject, and the women had written him care of the magazine for advice, not knowing that he was a convict. The prisoner responded, asserting his innocence of a bank robbery in Bedford, Michigan, in which a bystander had been shot. He told the women he had been convicted at the age of 18, largely on the testimony of an eyewitness, although a lie detector test had shown that he had been truthful in denying the accusation.

The women immediately became interested in the case, and Keeler was called on to make a second test, which strongly indicated Blazenzitz was telling the truth. Lawyers joined in a new investigation, and on the basis of their conclusions Blazenzitz was pardoned by the governor.

Keeler's former associates still recall the time that Governor Henry Horner of Illinois had him give an eleventh-hour test to a man facing the electric chair. The man was Joseph Rappaport, a 31-year-old dope peddler, sentenced to death for murdering an informant. Influential friends, moved by his emphatic pleas of innocence, had come to the man's defense and persuaded the governor five times to grant stays of execution pending further investigation.

Fifteen hours before the expiration of the last stay, Horner was confronted by a tearful woman, Rose Rappaport, the condemned man's sister, who came to plead for one more stay or a commutation of sentence. Touched by the woman's emotion and earnestness, Governor Horner told her that he had great faith in the ability of Leonarde Keeler, then of Northwestern University, and would call on him to give her brother a lie detector test. He said he would be guided by Keeler's findings.

Rose Rappaport grabbed at this one remaining chance and persuaded her brother's lawyer to request an order permitting the test. The plea was granted, and on March 1, 1937, Keeler arrived at the penitentiary; it was only four hours before Rappaport was to go to the chair.

Interrupting a pinochle game between the condemned man and his guards, Keeler and his associates filed into the prisoner's cell. Losing no time in completing the customary preparations, Keeler began as quickly as possible, opening, of course, with the usual innocuous questions:

"Is your name Rappaport?"

"Yes."

"Do you like cigars?"

"Yes."

"Did you kill Dent?"

"No."

"Were you present when he was killed?"

"No."

The questioning continued for more than an hour. When it was over, Keeler hastened to the governor's office, while clocks ticked off Rappaport's last hours on earth. When he showed Governor Horner the graphs, he said, "This man lied in answering my questions. On the basis of the test you requested, I'd say he's guilty."

Three hours later Rappaport was led to the electric chair.

Once Keeler examined the workers employed by a large retail chain that had lost $14,000 through dishonesty in one year. He found that 76 percent of the employees had been helping themselves to property that was not theirs. A similar test given a year later found the number of dishonest employees to be only 3 percent. The others, Keeler reasoned, could not bear the stigma of being detected.

Another remarkable case in Keeler's career involved the murder of Rose Gendler of Rock Island, Illinois. After an entire neighborhood had been subjected to lie detector tests, suspicion focused on Morris Myer. Sensing that he had "failed" the lie detector test, Myer fled and did not return until many months later when he thought the case would be forgotten. But the case had not been forgotten, and when he was asked to take another test, Myer confessed rather than undergo another examination.

Although Dr. John Larson, long deceased, cannot now recount any of his experiences and accomplishments with the earlier type of polygraph, his achievements are related in his book, *Lying and Its Detection,* written in collaboration with Leonarde Keeler and George W. Haney. Published in 1932, it is still used as a reference.

Larson, with the help of the lie detector, solved many mysteries and helped save the police much time and unnecessary work. One of his cases concerned a rash of petty thefts in a Berkeley boardinghouse near the campus. Police were being deluged with complaints from girls who were losing clothing, jewelry, and money. Suspicion turned to the landlady's daughter, who was known to be buying expensive clothing beyond her means.

Tested by Larson and exposed as a liar, the daughter confessed in the presence of her father and a police officer that she had stolen at every opportunity and had bought luxuries from stores with stolen money. She did it, she said, to improve her appearance in order to attract the interest of a boy with whom she was infatuated.

These and like results, achieved by experts throughout the country, explain why polygraphy is steadily gaining the support of those engaged in criminal justice. They explain as well why more and more people are enrolling in the training schools for potential lie detector examiners maintained by such men as Reid in Chicago, Backster in New York City, and Merit in Los Angeles. There are many such institutes in a number of states, and their enrollments increase steadily.

PART TWO

———

Cases
In Point

7

A Trick That Failed

I s it possible to fool the lie detector?

Experts agree that it is extremely difficult, especially if the examiner is experienced, alert, and efficient. Chester Weger of Illinois once thought he had succeeded, but he found himself trapped and received a life sentence in the penitentiary.

The crime occurred at Starved Rock State Park, a large wildlife recreation area in La Salle County, Illinois. The absorbing murder mystery began on the sunny afternoon of March 16, 1960, when a group of boys trudging through the park came upon the brutally bludgeoned corpses of three women. The bodies were partially obscured in a rugged cave beneath overhanging boulders.

A bloodied length of tree bough lying beside the bodies was obviously the murder weapon, but the motive remained a mystery for a considerable time. Investigation by state police turned first to an attempt to identify the victims. Through credit cards and personal papers found in their handbags, it was learned that the unfortunate trio had been staying for the past two days at the nearby Starved Rock Lodge. They were Mrs. Lillian Oetting, Mrs. Mildred Lindquist, and Mrs. Frances Murphy. All were middle-aged. Their husbands were prominent and affluent Chicago businessmen.

Later information disclosed that the women had left their

homes together in a station wagon driven by Mrs. Murphy, intending to spend a few days in the park. They had been observed the day before, walking from the lodge after lunch, headed in the direction of the cave where their remains were found.

An intensive investigation was soon under way by state police. But despite diligent effort, little progress was made. The mystery might never have been solved if not for the help of the lie detector and a highly trained operator who knew exactly how to use it.

Public criticism mounted as weeks and months slipped by with no meaningful result. People everywhere demanded the capture of the killer. Strangely, more scorn was heaped on the state's attorney for La Salle County, Harland D. Warren, a capable and long-experienced lawyer, than on the police. This was a peculiar and wholly inconsistent attitude, for Warren's responsibility was to assemble evidence gathered by the police and to present it convincingly to a jury. Capture of the brutal murderer would be the duty of the police, who in this case appeared to have been spared from public censure.

Warren and the police force had worked together from the start but had found themselves in total disagreement as to procedures. When officers failed in their efforts to find fingerprints on the lethal weapon and elsewhere, and when the absence of tangible clues became painfully apparent, the investigating officers concluded that the murders had likely been committed by Chicago gangsters invading new territory. Warren, however, held tenaciously to another and far different line of inquiry.

From the first, Warren had been deeply impressed by a strange aspect of the murders. Two of the women had been tied together by their ankles and wrists with strong white cord. The cord was tied with knots of an unusual character. The women's clothing had been pulled up over their waists and their undergarments had been torn to shreds, giving the impression of a sex crime. The cord and knots, Warren stoutly maintained, could be worthwhile clues. The police, however, shrugged their shoulders and told the prosecutor that he was mistaken.

Nevertheless, the police did round up sex deviates and other sex offenders recently discharged from prison, but all to no avail. Scores of the lodge's employees had also been questioned in vain. For a time, suspicion had turned to one former worker at the inn, a young man whose leather jacket was covered with stains that looked like blood. But the man satisfactorily explained that the red marks were the blood of a rabbit he had recently shot while hunting.

At Warren's request, however, the man was subjected to a lie detector test given by a somewhat inexperienced examiner, who was called on simply because he lived and worked in the vicinity. When the examiner reported that the polygraph results showed the suspect, Chester Weger, had been telling the truth, the police quickly abandoned their suspicions. The polygraphist's conclusion was strengthened by an expert's report that the blood on Weger's coat had indeed come from a rabbit.

For three months after the crime, Warren received biting criticism from all parts of Illinois. Realizing that his political career was at stake, he daringly decided to take the investigation into his own hands despite the fact that he had practically no experience as a criminal investigator.

His plans were influenced in part by his intention to attend the coming conference of the National District Attorney's Association in Boston, and he was counting on some of his colleagues at the meeting to come up with helpful suggestions as to procedure.

In Boston, Warren talked to others who agreed that the string and knots might well be important clues. They advised him to visit the waterfront and talk to seasoned seamen. This Warren did, and his theory soon gained support from seafaring men who assured him that the knots were of a type frequently used by those who followed the sea.

His early conjecture strengthened, Warren returned home and asked the sheriff to assign two deputies to assist him. Two aides, William Dummett and Wayne Hess, were instructed to work with the prosecutor. Warren was highly pleased with their selection, for while the two men were totally inexperienced in criminal investigation, both were hard-working officers who could be trusted to keep their work secret.

Their first assignment was to undertake a microscopic study of the little pieces of twine which had been used to bind the murder victims together. Laborious study revealed that most of the little fragments consisted of precisely twenty very thin strands of fiber, although a scant few contained only twelve strands.

"Where would this string have come from?" Warren asked his assistants as they contemplated their next move. Voicing his own opinion, Warren suggested checking at the lodge, for he firmly believed that the killer was an employee or a former worker there.

Searching every room of the lodge, the two deputies found many short lengths of string. Studied under the microscope, they all appeared exactly the same. Significantly, those comprising twenty strands came from the kitchen where the onetime suspect Chester Weger had been employed.

Warren's next step was to consult the lodge manager to obtain permission for a lie detector examination of not only every employee but of every former worker who could be located. This time, Warren decided, the examining polygraphist must be a man of nationally recognized ability and experience. He readily selected John Reid of Chicago, who agreed to undertake the assignment. Reid was soon on his way to Starved Rock Park, and a temporary workshop was set up there.

Lodge employees agreed to submit to polygraph examination. They were assured in advance that their participation in no way implied suspicion. And, in fact, all the tests thoroughly cleared the participants. The next step was to round up former lodge workers. This was no easy task for Hess and Dummett.

In due time they rounded up Chester Weger, who had already taken two lie detector tests and was now working in a La Salle suburb as a house painter to support his wife and two children. Although records showed that Weger, 21 years of age, had been cleared by the polygraph, he readily consented to subject himself to a third test.

Reid was prepared to follow his time-tested technique. As he prepared Weger for the third examination, he was disturbed by his subject's jocular manner and carefree laughter. Questioning had not proceeded long when Reid abruptly came to the point, demanding to know whether Weger was in fact the wanted murderer.

"Of course not," Weger fairly shouted, but this time the recording graph indicated that he was deliberately lying!

Reid's report to Warren was received with amazement. It was difficult to comprehend why this man, who twice before had been vindicated by the lie detector, should now be exposed as a liar.

"How do you account for such a situation?" Warren asked Reid.

"Simple enough," replied the Chicago expert. "It's all a matter of technique—in knowing how to conduct such an experiment effectively."

Still, Warren was not completely satisfied. It was finally decided to conduct a fourth test. This was done with similar results, and now Warren was no longer dubious. However, he realized that because no stipulation had been made, his lie detector evidence would not be admissible in court. He and the police would have to use the damning information in another way. After much deliberation, it was decided to keep Weger under close surveillance and to undertake an exhaustive but highly secret investigation of the man's background and movements on the day of the murders.

Surprising results followed. It was learned that Weger, despite his previous insistence that he had been far away from the park at the time of the murders, had actually been working there as a relief man. Next came an FBI chemist's findings that the red stains on Weger's leather jacket were really human and not rabbit blood.

Warren again turned his attention to the pieces of twine and the knots. He was troubled by the fact that the knots appeared to be the work of a seafaring man, yet Weger, as far as the prosecutor could learn, had never been to sea. But it was soon discovered that Weger had served in the Marines and was known for his ability to tie knots.

At this point, many a prosecutor would have ordered an arrest and risked a jury's reaction to his evidence—more or less circumstantial as it was—but not Warren. A meticulous lawyer, he always pictured himself before a jury and wondered how those in the box would react to his case. Now he asked himself how well prepared he was to disprove an alibi if Weger chose to insist on his original claim that he was away from the lodge at the time of the crime.

In the hope of finding a witness who had actually seen the suspect near the murder scene, Warren instructed the deputies to locate people who had been at the lodge that day, show them Weger's photograph, and ask if they had seen him. Days passed before they finally located a woman who recognized the picture as that of a young man she had observed hurrying away from the cave.

Again Warren pondered his next move, but other circumstances were to influence his decision. He was a candidate for reelection, and his opponent, a vigorous young lawyer knowing nothing of the progress of Warren's secret investigation, was making the most of the murder case. Should Warren order an arrest at this time, the move would be branded as a political gesture. Warren's major goal was to solve the mystery and convict the killer, so he continued to keep the investigation secret. As he feared, he was defeated at the polls, but the investigation went on as before. And now the defeated prosecutor was free to act without political considerations.

At last Warren sent a curt order to the deputies: "Bring Weger in. Do it as quietly as you can."

Warren had decided to defer questioning for several days, allowing time for Weger to struggle with his supposedly guilty conscience. And when he did confront his prisoner, Warren was determined to tell him everything he knew. When they finally sat face to face, Warren recounted all the results of his long investigation, sparing no details. His recital left Weger pale and nervous, squirming in his chair, and moving his fingers in a way that betrayed his emotions. A break seemed imminent.

"Now you've heard my story, Weger," Warren said in conclusion. "Let's hear yours—and let it be the truth this time."

Weger's face blanched, and he wet his lips. "You've got me cold," he finally blurted. "I'll tell you the truth this time."

County officials and a stenographer were summoned and the

apparently relieved Weger began relating the grim details. He said he had been heavily in debt and had gone to the park intent on purse snatching. He had seen his three victims ambling along and concluded they would be easy prey—his first mistake.

Mrs. Murphy, carrying a camera with a strap over her shoulder, was his first victim. He seized her camera strap, thinking it was fastened to a handbag, but the woman resisted. Still with no thought of murder, Weger told the trio to walk ahead toward the cave. He followed them at a distance, and as they walked he began to look for a weapon. The tree bough lay on the ground; it was exactly what he needed. Holding it before the frightened women, he ordered them to lie down on the ground. After they obeyed, he bound them with the twine, which he had taken from the kitchen of the lodge.

"Then I started taking their money and jewelry," Weger recounted, "but I didn't expect a fight. One of them, the one with the camera, broke loose and hit me a nasty one over the head. I reached for that tree bough and let her have it.

"By this time, the others had more or less freed themselves, and I knew I was in for it. I knew they'd report me. That was the first moment that murder came into my mind, and I thought of nothing but saving myself. I struck them over their heads again and again until they lay still. Yes, I even took their pulses to make sure that they were gone.

"There was nothing to do but drag the bodies into the cave, and after that I beat it fast. The rest you know."

Warren had many questions before he finally asked Weger how he had fooled the lie detector in the first two tests.

For the first time Weger laughed. "That," he boasted, "was the easiest of all. Before those tests, I just swallowed a lot of aspirin and washed it down with a bottle of Coke. That calms a guy down, you know. Why I didn't do that before this other guy tested me I'll never know."

Now Warren had still one more question to ask. "Tell me, Weger," he demanded, "why did you drag those ladies into the cave after you'd killed them? We found plenty of drag marks on the soft ground."

Weger explained that just as he was turning from the murder

scene he observed a red-and-white Piper plane flying overhead and thought the pilot might be a policeman searching for the women.

Realizing the importance of that statement, Warren suddenly jumped to his feet. If it could be verified, he would have a vital piece of corroborative evidence. Dummett, a former Air Force flier, was the first to help. He explained to Warren that Piper planes fly a radius of between 250 and 300 miles an hour.

"Okay," the lawyer exclaimed, "now here's where both of you, Dummett and Hess, start on a new job. Get a map and draw a circle with a two-hundred-fifty-mile radius from Ottawa airport. Then visit every airport within that circle. Your job will be to ascertain whether a Piper, red and white, was flying over that area on the day of the murder. Follow me?"

The deputies nodded.

At Ottawa airport they observed a similar plane on the ground. It was not a Piper but a model bearing close resemblance. They learned that it was the property of contractor Homer Charbonneau, who always parked it there. But had it been aloft on March 16, 1960, the day of the murders? The owner's log would tell. Fortunately, the log was on file at the airport, and it disclosed that Charbonneau had actually flown over Starved Rock Park at the exact time Weger claimed to have seen the plane.

Warren, now fully satisfied that he had developed an airtight case, presented it to the grand jury. Weger was indicted on three murder charges. But the following week, Weger repudiated his confession, insisting that he had admitted the triple murders only under duress. Warren was neither surprised nor perturbed.

A jury of five men and seven women was sworn to try the case in the court of Judge Leonard Hoffman. The prosecution, of course, was in the hands of the new district attorney, but Warren was kept busy organizing the evidence. Naturally he felt a glow of satisfaction in view of the criticism that had been heaped upon him. More than fifty witnesses were called to the stand, each adding a strong link to the chain of evidence against the accused.

Weger himself was the principal witness for the defense.

Under direct examination by his attorney, Joseph Carr, he categorically denied every part of the confession, insisting on his innocence and contending he had been coached by the prosecution.

Asked if he had been told to mention the red-and-white plane, he said he had, but the prosecutor grasped the opportunity to tell the jury that nothing had been known about this until the defendant himself mentioned it to the investigators. On Weger's 22nd birthday, March 4, 1961, the jury retired. Nine hours elapsed before it returned to the courtroom with a verdict: Guilty. "We recommend," read the foreman, "that he be imprisoned for the remainder of his life." The jurors, it was later learned, had taken seven ballots to reach their decision; all the jurors except one had voted for the death penalty.

There was talk of an appeal by the defense, but the plan was soon dropped and Weger was taken to Statesville Penitentiary.

Warren was deluged with congratulations on his achievement, and a short time later his fellow citizens, including some who had once been his severest critics, showed their gratitude by electing him to the Illinois State Legislature.

Twenty-one-year-old Jorge Martinez of Florida earned himself a place beside Chester Weger of Illinois for his ability to fool the lie detector. How he did it has never been explained, but he fared better than Weger—he escaped a prison sentence.

Despite his youth, Jorge was manager of a store in the little town of Hialeah, Florida, a community of some 70,000. He earned a fair salary, but apparently it was not enough to meet the needs of the ambitious young man.

Early one bright fall morning in October, 1970, Martinez walked into the executive offices of his employers in the Tom Thumb store with a startling story. "I was held up and robbed here in the store late last night," he said. "And I'm sorry that I couldn't prevent them from taking so much of your money."

"What happened?" his bosses asked.

"I was working very late and had just cleared my desk long after we'd closed the store when two men walked in. I'd·never seen them before, and they had guns in their hands. They told me to lie down on the floor, and while I lay there helpless they emptied the cash register of all we'd taken in during the last three days."

"How much did they get?" asked one of the store owners.

"Fifteen thousand dollars," Martinez answered. "You see, I hadn't had time to get to the bank."

"And did you call the police?" he was asked.

"Of course I did," he quickly replied, "and they searched the whole neighborhood but couldn't find any trace of the men I'd described."

The police were called again, and there was a long conference between them and the store owners. Some thought that Martinez' story sounded fishy; officers had detected a few striking discrepancies in his report. One officer suggested that the robbery sounded like an inside job. And Jorge Martinez, a detective observed, seemed to be spending more than he earned.

The young man was called in and questioned. He retold his story and seemed offended that anyone should doubt his word. One of his employers later proposed that he take a lie detector test, and Martinez agreed to do so.

"Let's get a really good lie detector expert," one of the Tom Thumb owners urged. "Someone we can rely on."

A nationally know specialist was summoned; his name—perhaps it should be forgotten. When the test was over, the examiner reported that the graph conclusively showed Martinez to be telling the truth.

The report was a welcome one, for the store proprietors had full trust in Martinez; in fact, he had risen to his present position from an errand boy. One of them even recommended calling the young man in and apologizing for making him submit to the lie detector test.

"Don't be in such a hurry," admonished Detective Fred Kemper, who had been sitting with the others. "That young fellow is pulling your leg. Before you do any apologizing, let me have a try at him. To me this looks exactly like an inside job. I'd like to have a few minutes alone with him. Maybe I can get the truth."

No one objected, and young Martinez accompanied the shrewd detective to police headquarters. Kemper, hero of many a crime mystery, chose to be brutally frank. He told the young manager that he disbelieved his story. "That lie detector report doesn't fool me," he began. "Why don't you start by telling me the truth?"

"I've already told it all to you," Martinez angrily replied.

"Well try again," snapped the officer. "I wasn't born yesterday."

Jorge Martinez squirmed in his chair, and color rose in his cheeks.

"Just the truth now, Jorge," Detective Kemper repeated. "You haven't fooled me. There really wasn't any holdup, was there?" Pointing an accusing finger, the officer again demanded, "Come clean."

Now the young manager pulled out his handkerchief and daubed his forehead. "All right," he finally spluttered. "I took the money because I needed it. No, there really wasn't any holdup."

"And who was in on the job with you?" Kemper demanded.

"Carlos Nunez," Martinez whispered. "He gave me courage. We planned it all together."

An hour later Martinez and the 38-year-old Nunez occupied adjoining cells, both charged with grand theft. And a few days later, the two stood before Judge Murray Goodman and pleaded guilty. They said that they were ready for sentence.

From the bench Judge Goodman looked down at young Martinez. "I'm going to give you another chance," he told the pale-faced young man. "You'll be on probation for the next three years." Nunez received the same sentence.

Detective Kemper smiled modestly when he returned to the store to report the court's results to the owners. "I'm telling you," he remarked, "those lie detectors can't detect anything. The polygraph machine is merely an investigative aid even when administered by someone as expert as the man who made this examination."

The Schwartz Mystery

During their careers with the Berkeley Police Department, Chief Vollmer and Dr. Larson solved many fascinating cases with the help of the lie detector. But perhaps none was more interesting than the first cases in which the polygraph was used effectively. It all began when Charles Henry Schwartz, a chemist, startled industrialists and men of science by claiming that he had developed a formula for making artificial silk. He claimed to have the backing of wealthy financiers.

To put his formula into practical use, Mr. Schwartz established a pseudo plant in the quiet little town of Walnut Creek on the eastern side of San Francisco Bay. The place attracted considerable attention, and Schwartz, contending that he needed to protect his secret, kept the public away and maintained a twenty-four-hour guard.

Schwartz might have continued his deceit had not the "factory" been rocked by a destructive explosion on the night of July 30, 1925. The blast shook the entire neighborhood and was followed by a roaring fire that completely enveloped the building. Flames and smoke were billowing into the skies when firemen arrived, and it was quickly apparent that they could do nothing to save the plant. Donning masks and carrying hoses, they forced their way inside, fearing that someone might be trapped there. The ground floor was vacant, but, risking their lives, they fought their way up a burning stairway to check the main laboratory. There they encountered a peculiar yellowish gas. On the floor lay the badly burned body of a man, charred entirely beyond recognition. Forced by smoke and heat to retreat, the firemen then confined their efforts to trying to keep the flames from spreading to nearby property.

Long afterward, when the structure had been reduced to little more than a charred skeleton, a terrified man elbowed his way through the crowd, apparently determined to enter the smoldering building. "Who are you, and what do you want?" a deputy sheriff demanded. "Get back or you'll get killed."

The stranger excitedly explained that he was Walter Gonzales, Schwartz' assistant and the night watchman. "I'm afraid Mr. Schwartz was burned to death in the fire," he said.

"There is a burned body upstairs," the deputy said. "Perhaps it's Mr. Schwartz."

"I must see for myself," answered Gonzales, now close to a state of hysteria. "Can't I go up and look at the body?"

Permission was reluctantly granted on condition that Gonzales return to safety as soon as possible. A fireman accompanied him. After one look at the charred remains, Gonzales asserted that he was certain the body was that of his employer. "Poor, unfortunate man," he sobbed. "Only a short while ago I left him here and now. . . ."

As he reached the street, Gonzales was met by Sheriff R. R. Veale, who had reached the scene with a party of deputies and was trying to ascertain whether the explosion and fire were caused by accident or arson. His first suspicion fell on Gonzales.

"If you're the watchman, why did you leave the place unguarded?" the sheriff demanded.

"That I can easily explain," said Gonzales. "Mr. Schwartz told me to go get my supper, that he was working on an experiment and wanted to be alone. So I went around the corner to eat, and now—the poor man was horribly trapped."

Veale and his men were in a suspicious mood, however. Some were far from satisfied with Gonzales' explanation. Others wondered whether the body was really that of Schwartz; a few were anxious about the manner of death and the cause of the explosion. Huddled together in serious conversation, they were approached by a woman who said she was Mrs. Schwartz and that she wanted to see the body at once. They escorted her upstairs into the burned laboratory. One look at the remains and she shrieked: "Take me out of here!"

This somewhat satisfied Veale as to identification, but he was unwilling to eliminate Gonzales as a suspect. "What would he have to gain by killing his boss and setting fire to the place?" he wondered aloud. "He'd certainly lose his job."

"That's easy to answer," said one deputy. "Maybe he wanted that secret formula for himself. Perhaps Schwartz had money in his pockets or in the till. Who knows?"

Veale, still not totally satisfied that a correct identification had been made, ordered the funeral deferred for a few days, a move that brought bitter protests from Schwartz' widow, relatives, and friends. Mrs. Schwartz angrily called the sheriff's action an outrage and insisted that her husband had been murdered.

The authorities, however, were far from agreed. "It really could have been suicide," reasoned one of the investigators. His surmise was predicated on his discovery that Schwartz had recently been sued for breach of promise by an attractive young woman employed in a Walnut Creek beauty salon. "Could be," this man suggested, "that he was troubled by the suit and deliberately set fire to his factory only to be trapped there."

Suspicion against Gonzales continued nevertheless. He was questioned again and although he repeatedly denied any responsibility for the fire, he failed to convince the officers that he was telling the truth.

Soon a new idea came from one of the deputies. "If Gonzales *is* innocent," he asked, "could the murderer, whoever he was, have planned this thing in a way to deliberately throw suspicion on the watchman?"

"That's an idea worth considering," said Veale. "Why don't we phone Chief Vollmer and get him over here? He could be of great help to us."

They phoned the Berkeley police chief at his office. Less than an hour later Vollmer was on the scene, listening to all of the conjecture that had been going on. He quickly came up with a suggestion. "If you're not completely satisfied that this watchman Gonzales is in the clear," he said, "why don't you suggest that he take a lie detector test? Whatever the outcome," he was quick to add, "it can't be admissible in court, but at least it will tell you if you're working in the right direction."

Vollmer followed with another question. "Tell me," he asked, "why do you really suspect this man?"

"For several good reasons," a deputy replied. "For one thing, he was the last to see Schwartz alive; for another, he had much to gain by Schwartz' death, and . . ."

Vollmer nodded. "Why doesn't someone talk to Gonzales," he said. "Let's find out how he feels about a lie detector test."

Gonzales, obviously shaken by the suspicion of the others, had no objections. "Of course I'll take a test," he told Vollmer. "Why shouldn't I? All I want is a chance to clear myself to your satisfaction. The sooner the better."

Vollmer called his Berkeley office and summoned his best polygraph expert, directing him to be in readiness on the following morning.

When the test was over, the expert reported that the watchman had given convincing and truthful answers to every question. Vollmer, who had been present during the test, agreed that it had been conclusive in every way. Gonzales breathed a sigh of relief and offered to assist the investigation in every way possible. No doubt he realized the full meaning of his vindication—that he had been spared not only the stigma of a murder accusation but also the necessity of spending all his scant savings for a defense with unforeseen results. Yet he could not have imagined the strange and bizarre ending of the case.

Vollmer, resorting to his expertise and long experience in crime detection, pointed out that in his judgment the next logical move would be to determine whether the burned body was actually that of Schwartz. "And if it is not Schwartz," he stated, "we'd better find out pretty quickly just whose body it is. That may very well help us to determine whether this was an accident or a crime."

As the inquiry progressed, new and puzzling information came to light, pointing to a new line of investigation. Veale learned that only a short time before the fire, Schwartz had insured his life for $185,000, insisting that the policy cover accidental death.

Insurance company records added a still more significant revelation—the burned body was three inches taller than Schwartz.

Schwartz' personal physician had viewed the remains and was certain beyond doubt that the dead man was his patient. Business associates were equally positive. After examining a watch and other jewelry found on the body, they said that these positively had belonged to the chemist.

The inquiry, still focused on identification, led to Schwartz' dentist after the coroner reported that "an upper right" molar was missing. Checking his charts, the dentist found that he had extracted such a tooth from Schwartz' mouth only months before. This appeared to eliminate any remaining doubt that Schwartz had been the victim, but new and still more confusing facts came to light, adding new mystery to the case.

Mrs. Esther Hatfield, who had been Schwartz' private secretary, told police that shortly before the fire broke out, she had seen Schwartz put $900 in currency in his pocket. No burned greenbacks had been found on the body, however. Even more puzzling was a belated report to the sheriff by the widow, who complained that only hours before the explosion her home had been entered during her absence. "I can't understand it," she said. "Money and jewelry left on my bureau were not touched, but every photograph of my husband—and there were several in a number of rooms—was taken away."

More than a week had passed since the fire, and the investigators were facing a maze of puzzling and conflicting developments. Veale and Vollmer sat down at a conference with a number of deputies to review the case and to chart a new and hopefully more effective course of inquiry. They decided to enlist the services of a pioneer criminalist of Berkeley, Edward Oscar Heinrich, who was known to have solved many baffling mysteries.

Heinrich, often called on for help by federal, state, and local authorities, accepted the challenge and agreed to meet with officials the following day in Walnut Creek. His first question, which he posed after jotting down copious notes pertaining to the investigation, caused some raised eyebrows among those present. "If you think the victim was Schwartz," he began, "find out for me what he ate for his supper the night of the explosion."

At that point, an officer said he had been informed that Schwartz' last meal had consisted of beans and cucumbers.

Heinrich made a note of this before requesting that one of Schwartz' hairbrushes, one of the last he had used, be obtained and sent to Heinrich's laboratory as quickly as possible. "You'll hear from me shortly," he promised.

Two days passed before Heinrich reported by telephone. "I have some news that will come to you as a surprise," he told Veale. "First of all, the dead man is not Schwartz. Of that I am certain."

"How can you be so positive so soon?" Sheriff Veale inquired almost incredulously.

"For a number of very definite reasons," Heinrich retorted. "First of all," he began, "the autopsy surgeon says that there was only meat in the dead man's stomach—not the slightest trace of beans or cucumbers. Secondly, I compared a few hairs from the brush with samples I'd clipped from the body. No similarity whatsoever."

"But what about that missing tooth?" the Sheriff inquired. "I told you what the dentist said."

"You certainly did," replied Heinrich, "but I did a microscopic examination there. The victim's tooth wasn't extracted; it was carefully knocked out by someone using a chisel. I saw the root still imbedded in the gum. That dead man was murdered, you can be sure of that; and if you doubt my word, let me assure you that I discovered a wound on the back of the head—a wound obviously caused by a blunt instrument. Someone obviously murdered this man—whoever he was—and took meticulous pains to make certain that the body would be identified as Schwartz. Wait for me—I'm on my way over."

Heinrich, a chemist and an expert in the field of physics, had examined the burned laboratory inch by inch in the hope of ascertaining the cause of the explosion. Following the theory that Schwartz, a chemist with many years of experience, might have used every trick of his profession to make the blast appear accidental, he'd gathered samples of charred wood and other materials, including the residue of what appeared to have been a liquid.

After many hours of work in his own laboratory, Heinrich concluded that the floor of Schwartz' lab had been soaked with a highly flammable liquid which had been ignited from the outside. Still more surprising was his disclosure of blood stains which indicated that the dead man, definitely not Schwartz, had been murdered outside the building and then dragged to the spot where the body was found. Everything had been planned for deception, so that the corpse with Schwartz' watch and jewelry would be mistakenly identified as the chemist.

Heinrich's conclusions impressed the Walnut Creek authorities, but they agreed that one major question still remained unanswered. "You've solved half of our problem," Sheriff Veale told the criminologist. "Now, if the murdered man wasn't Schwartz, who in the world was he? How can we find out?"

Heinrich smiled. "I think I'm on the trail of that one. Hopefully, I should have the answer in a very few days."

"Give now," demanded District Attorney A. B. Tinning, who had joined the others interviewing Heinrich.

Heinrich adjusted his large, rimless spectacles and said, "I have reason to believe that the victim was an itinerant of some sort and . . ."

"What convinced you of that?" Tinning interrupted cautiously.

"A lot of things," said Heinrich. "For one, there was a bar of soap near the body—why would Schwartz use soap in a place without running water—and some other facts, too."

"Like what?" the sheriff asked.

"Fragments of burned clothing found near the remains were of blue denim, small bits of overalls and a hunting jacket—clothing that Schwartz, a fastidious dresser, never would have worn. And I found a needle and thread, even a bag of coffee—things that Schwartz with a wife and home never would have needed in his lab."

None of the investigators now doubted Heinrich's positive conclusion that Schwartz had murdered a man with a blow to the head and had arranged for the explosion, carefully setting the stage so the body would be identified as his own.

As a result, a warrant was issued for Schwartz' arrest for

murder. The hunt became nationwide. In fact, one newly discovered witness insisted that he had seen the wanted man driving away from the factory in a new high-powered car.

The search had been under way for only a few days when Heinrich came forward with another surprise. He was now positive that the victim had been an itinerant evangelist. Carefully studying a few scraps of charred paper found on the laboratory floor and treating them with chemicals, he was satisfied that they were part of a page of a religious tract, one containing excerpts from St. John. One fragment bore a line of handwriting, which at Heinrich's request was reproduced in a local newspaper.

In the old town of Placerville, far north of Sacramento, an undertaker named Barker viewed the reproduction of the script and quickly identified it as the singular writing of his friend Gilbert Warren Barbe, a traveling missionary. Viewing the body, which had already been moved to San Francisco, the mortician positively identified it as his friend Barbe. With Barker's help, the evangelist's wife was located. Tearfully she recognized the sewing kit as one she had given her husband.

Barbe, it developed, had a flair for chemistry and had accepted a job from Schwartz as a laboratory assistant. The two resembled each other, so the hapless evangelist was the ideal victim for Schwartz' diabolical plot.

But where was Schwartz?

While the hunt was at its height, a resident of Oakland, N. B. Edmonds, saw a picture of the wanted man in a newspaper. It bore a striking resemblance to a tenant in his apartment house, a man who called himself Harold Warren. Edmonds lost no time in confiding his suspicions to Captain Clarence Lee.

Quickly organizing a posse, Lee and his men hastened to the apartment building on Forty-first Street in Oakland, where manager C. W. Heywood directed them to the second-floor suite occupied by "Mr. Warren."

The police hurried to the second floor, taking the stairs two at a time. With gun in hand, Captain Lee pounded heavily on the apartment door. "We're the police," he shouted. "Open up and come out with your hands up."

There was no response.

Lee repeated his command. "If you don't come out, we'll break down your door," he added.

The posse waited tensely, guns at the ready.

Suddenly they heard a shot inside.

"Let's go," Lee commanded.

Powerful shoulders pressed hard against the wooden door. There was a creak, the sound of splintering wood, and the door suddenly flew open. On the floor lay Schwartz with a bullet hole in his head and an automatic clutched in his hand. The long hunt was over. A pathetic farewell note addressed to his wife lay on a hall table.

A few days later a small knot of friends attended the funeral. Among them was Gonzales, the watchman, shocked by the tragedy but thankful that the lie detector had spared him from suspicion and from what might have been a far more serious consequence.

Banning Broken Promises

I t was an unusual decision in a most extraordinary case. In effect, the Supreme Court of Michigan ruled that a prosecutor must keep his word with a defendant just as anyone else is morally bound to honor a promise. As a result of the high court's judgment, defendant E. J. Reagan walked out of the courthouse a free man after two lie detector tests had indicated that he was not culpable for the heinous crime of which he was accused.

In a face-to-face conference with the defendant and his lawyer, the prosecutor had promised to dismiss charges if the results of a polygraph examination by state police were favorable to Reagan. Reagan took the test and passed but the prosecutor tried to renege on the agreement. Consequently, Reagan carried his case to Michigan's highest court.

The case had a strange beginning in early 1971, when Reagan was arrested on a charge of "torturing a child and of assault to do great bodily harm less than murder." Specifically, the accusation was that Reagan, while acting as a baby-sitter, had immersed the feet of the child in very hot water, causing serious injury. Reagan, however, contended that he had acted in good faith and without criminal intent; that he conscientiously believed he had acted in the best interest of the child, who was seriously ill with a cold.

While awaiting trial, Reagan subjected himself to a lie

detector test given privately by a Sergeant Sparks. According to Sparks, it showed that Reagan was telling the truth and "that the injury was at most the result of the defendant's negligence."

Attorney P. C. Flint, representing Reagan, hastened to bring these findings to the attention of the prosecutor's office, and it was agreed that the charges would be dismissed if Reagan passed a second polygraph examination administered by state police.

The defendant and his counsel fully agreed to that condition, and Reagan underwent a second test, this one given by Ralph E. Cabot of the Michigan State Police. Cabot's conclusions were similar to those of the first polygraphist. Supporting these findings was the opinion of two reputable physicians, Drs. Conlan and Schappach, who stated that the child's injuries could have occurred just as the accused man claimed they had.

Believing that the terms of the agreement with the prosecutor had been fulfilled, Reagan's attorney demanded that the promise be kept. Accordingly, an assistant prosecutor called upon the court to approve an order of nolle prosequi, which would mean dismissal of charges without prejudice but would not preclude initiation of subsequent prosecution. Such an order promptly came from the court.

The defense was gratified, regarding the court action vindicating Reagan as nothing more than a fulfillment of the original understanding. But the prosecutor, calling the lie detector tests unreliable and inconclusive, was far from satisfied. He and his aides believed they had a legal right to reopen the case to satisfy themselves. They met with a psychiatrist from the Center for Forensic Psychiatry and were told that if Reagan had deliberately tried to burn the child's feet, he might be a schizophrenic—and that a schizophrenic nature will sometimes distort psychiatric test results. In that case, the doctor suggested, serum tests would be more likely to "get at the truth."

This suggestion was spurned by the state's counsel, and a new complaint similar to the one that had been dismissed was filed. The defense protested bitterly and moved to quash the new charges on the basis of the earlier agreement, but the court refused. It did, however, acknowledge the existence of the now-repudiated verbal contract. In so doing, the court ruled that in no way was Reagan "prejudiced" by withdrawal of the agreement and the filing of a new and like complaint.

Consequently, Reagan was rearrested and arraigned. He remained silent when asked by the judge if he were guilty, and a "Not guilty" plea was entered for him, after which we was formally bound over to the higher court for trial.

The jury convicted him, and he promptly filed an appeal which was denied by the Court of Appeals. This judgment was then carried to the State Supreme Court of Michigan, which finally found in Reagan's favor in a notable decision written by Justice Fitzgerald.

In effect, the decision was a slap on the wrist for the prosecutor's office for reneging on the agreement. It directed that the complaint against Reagan be dismissed. Accordingly he became a free and vindicated man.

The significance of the opinion analyzing the essential elements of the case, as written by Justice Fitzgerald, warrants repetition here largely because of its language, its reasoning, and its intimate interpretation of the delicate issues involved. Said the court:

> The principal issue on this appeal concerns the binding effect of an agreement entered into by the defendant and the Genesee County prosecutor's office, to dismiss prosecution if the defendant passed a polygraph examination. The defendant passed the polygraph examination. Pursuant to the agreement, the prosecutor sought an order of nolle prosequi. Such an order was approved by the trial court. The prosecutor's office then reneged on the acknowledged agreement and reinstated prosecution, having obtained information indicating that the polygraph examination of the defendant may have been unreliable. Defendant was subsequently convicted of child torture. . . .
>
> We conclude that the prosecutor's office in entering into the agreement with defendant, gave a pledge of public faith which became binding when nolle prosequi order was approved by the trial judge. Defendant is discharged.

The decision then relates the circumstances of Reagan's arrest, the details of his agreement with the prosecutor's office, his successful passing of two polygraph tests, dismissal of the case, the subsequent filing of a new complaint, and the defendant's conviction by a jury. The judgment resumes:

> Subsequent to the foregoing events, the prosecutor's office entertained serious misgivings about the polygraph test results, given the 'compelling circumstantial evidence' of defendant's criminal involvement.

The judgment continues with a review of the circumstances of a prosecutor's visit to the psychiatric center which resulted in the proposal that Reagan undergo a serum test. It continues:

> In the present case the reasons presented by the prosecutor in support of the nolle prosequi were that defendant had passed two polygraph tests and that his innocence was compatible with the testimony of two doctors. No record review as contemplated by Genesee prosecutor was apparently had in this case. There is no evidence that the judge took note of the 'evidence filed in the case' for purposes of reviewing prosecutorial discretion. The judge was never made aware of the agreement of the prosecutor with defendant.
>
> While the entry of the order of nolle prosequi cannot be said to approve an agreement never presented to the court, entry of the order represented necessary fruition of the agreement and approval of its stated basis as a matter of law and fact. . . .
>
> We take judicial notice of the fact that polygraph use by prosecutor's office, principally prior to the issuance of a complaint, is not uncommon and indeed is a useful investigatory device though its use is not approved at trial. Prosecutorial use of polygraph test results at any stage of the proceedings necessarily has the effect of supplanting the trial process. This is particularly so, as here, the prosecution dismissed after a preliminary examination, a determination that there was probably reason to believe that the crime charged was committed.
>
> We cannot commend the wisdom of the action taken by the prosecution and the judge in this case. Ordinarily use of polygraph test results should not occur after judicial proceedings have been instituted.

The role of the bargaining relationship between the people and their bargaining agent [the prosecutor]and a defendant charged with crime is not generally recognized.

The disposition of criminal charges by agreement between the prosecutor and accused, sometimes loosely called plea bargaining is an essential component of the administration of justice. Properly administered, it is to be encouraged. If every criminal charge were subjected to a full-scale trial, the states and the federal government would need to multiply by many times the number of judges and court facilities. . . .

Most courts which have considered the bargaining relationship have done so in the context of a plea-bargain situation. We agree with the people that this case presents atypical circumstances. No plea was the subject of bargain here. Defendant had much to gain and little to lose by subjecting himself to the polygraph. The people contend that the bargain offered defendant was a 'gift type' bargain which lacked the consideration necessary to make it binding. While there is precedential reference to the concept of 'consideration' for a bargain in the context of the administration of criminal justice, we feel that here the analogy to contract law is inappropriate. The standards of commerce do not govern the administration of criminal justice.

Citing a significant case, the court then points to *State v. Davis* in Florida in which the defendant was indicted for first degree murder, pleaded not guilty, and entered into a "bargain" with the prosecution whereby the defendant agreed to take a polygraph test administrated by an appointed examiner; if the polygraph showed the defendant to be telling the truth, the case against him would be dismissed, but if the test showed he was not telling the truth he would enter a plea of guilty to the lesser charge of manslaughter.

After the test, the examiner reported that he believed the defendant had told the truth. A second polygraphist was called on to give another test, and he disagreed with the earlier findings. Under these conditions the state refused to dismiss the indictment, and the defendant moved to quash on the basis of the agreement. The Florida court, however, found the agreement enforceable, stating that it was "a pledge of public faith—a promise made by state officials and one which should not be lightly disregarded."

Apparently the court believed that the findings of the first examiner were sufficient. Nevertheless the Michigan Supreme Court concluded its judgment with these words:

> Law enforcement processes are committed to civilized courses of action. When mistakes of significant proportion are made, it is better that the consequences be suffered than that civilized standards be sacrificed.

10

Cupid and the Lie Detector

Many people believe that the lie detector, because of its name, only reveals lies. But there are exceptions. This is a story about a very true and significant exception, and though many years have passed since it occurred, it deserves telling again.

The story began when an attractive young coed at the University of California in Berkeley called on the police to report that an alarming amount of pilfering was going on in a girls' dormitory on campus. Her name then was Margaret Taylor.

"I am really doing what all of the ninety girls in our dormitory didn't want anyone to do," she said with a show of embarrassment. "We had hoped that this could be solved without the police knowing about it. The university authorities wanted to handle this secretly, but that hasn't worked. Lots of things like jewelry, clothes, books, and even money are disappearing from the house, and we can't find the guilty person."

"Who's we?" asked the desk sergeant.

"That I'd rather not answer," Miss Taylor said. "But I can tell you that the authorities at the university would rather not have this become a police problem. We do not want publicity, but this thing really can't go on."

Moving through proper channels, the young woman's report soon reached Officer William Wiltberger, whose beat was the campus and who had secretly solved many a mystery involving students. Wiltberger got the assignment with a caution to avoid notoriety, but all of his efforts were to no avail. Methodically he visited pawnshops, old book stores, and other such places, trying to ascertain whether any of the missing articles had been pawned or sold. Not a clue turned up. Then he questioned the girls themselves, all of whom came from affluent families. As he had expected, they explained that they enjoyed liberal allowances and had no need to steal. In the end, the campus officer was obliged to report failure.

Before long, however, Miss Taylor's complaint reached Chief Vollmer, who always insisted that every report of crime on the campus be brought to his personal attention. Officer Wiltberger was summoned by the chief to discuss the vexing problem they were facing.

Vollmer's quick mind turned to one of his patrolmen, 23-year-old John Larson, whose work in criminology at Berkeley had earned him a master's degree. Larson had been delving into psychiatry, biology, physiology, and kindred subjects. He was also experimenting with a lie detecting instrument, which Larson had invented and was trying to use in the course of his regular police work.

"I'd suggest," Vollmer told Larson, "that you take that lie detecting instrument you're experimenting with to the dormitory and test every one of the girls living there. You can never tell; it well might pay off. Anyway, this will be your first important use of your invention, and I have faith in your lie detector."

Larson, not too pleased with the assignment, went to the dormitory and asked the girls if they would object to being examined by the polygraph. They were all willing.

Larson decided to first test Margaret Taylor. Since she had made the complaint to the police, he reasoned, she would logically be the last person to suspect. First he described to her the workings of his new equipment. He explained how the graph pens recorded heart beats, blood pressure, and respiration and how deviations would occur if the subject experienced emotional stress in answering the questions. She seemed interested and asked many questions. In fact, he found the conversation so enjoyable that he was moved to overlook the "control questions" he had previously prepared—innocuous questions like "What kind of movies do you prefer?" or "Which is your favorite subject?" Instead, he spent an hour or so in casual conversation which revealed Miss Taylor to be one of the most fascinating girls he had ever met—vivacious and intelligent, deeply interested in many subjects. She seemed intrigued by Larson's explanation of his own duties and the instrument he had invented. This was no ordinary coed, he told himself. Never before could he recollect meeting such a person, and he was sorry when the time came for the lie detector test itself.

As he had expected, the graph showed that all of her responses to key and pertinent questions concerning the thefts were truthful. He even broadened his interrogation to include words directly referring to the pilfering—questions containing the words "crime," "stealing," "purses," etc. All of her answers proved to be truthful, but her manner of speaking intrigued him; just why he could not really understand.

Testing of others continued for several days. In no instance could Larson detect lying, and the more he conversed with different students, the more he regretted that he was not still talking to Margaret Taylor. He was finally approached by Officer Wiltberger, who wanted to know how the investigation was going.

"Catch any of them lying?" he inquired.

"Just one or two—trivial sorts of fibs." Larson told him. "The questions did not seem to be very important."

"Most girls stretch their imaginations a bit," the officer said laughing. "Just don't be too suspicious. You may even have to test some of them a second time."

"A splendid idea," said Larson, as a vision of the attractive Miss Taylor flashed through his mind. "Suppose you ask that Miss Taylor to come in again."

Minutes later Margaret Taylor walked into the room with a quizzical look on her face. "I thought you'd told me that I had passed," she said. "Now what's wrong?"

"Nothing," Larson replied, "but I've got a new question here that's not on the list I first prepared."

"Shoot; I'm ready."

"Here it is on this paper," he told her. "Read it very slowly, and I'm warning you now that it demands a very truthful answer."

Margaret scanned the question and blushed. Larson's eyes were glued to the recording pens and her lips moved impishly without words. Then to his dismay he heard her swiftly spoken "No." But the lie detector's answer was the one for which he had hoped. He was convinced that she was lying. She repeated the same response, but the graph pens jerked violently.

"The machine definitely shows a dishonest, false reply," he told her. "I'm asking it again, and this time I want to hear only the truth."

Now the answer was a positive "Yes," as the girl, still blushing, inquired: "May I ask you the same question and get an equally truthful answer?"

Larson nodded and loudly answered "Yes." The all-important question was: "Do you love me?" The same responses, repeated many times, brought them together a year later before the altar. This time a clergyman pronounced them man and wife.

Long before, Larson had trapped the guilty girl who confessed and told him where she had hidden her booty. And not too long afterward, Dr. Larson, a nationally recognized leader in the field of lie detection, wrote his impressions and experiences in a book, called *Lying and Its Deception*. It proved to be a big seller and Margaret Larson displayed it proudly to her friends.

Infidelity and Employee Honesty

Contrary to general belief, the use of lie detectors is not confined to criminal investigations. They are used extensively and effectively to check employee honesty, to uncover "leaks" in industrial operations, and to resolve domestic disputes.

Many polygraph firms in the United States employ large staffs and provide various types of service. One of the largest and most influential, operating for more than half a century, is Merit Protective Service, Inc., with executive offices in Los Angeles and branches in many cities, including San Francisco, San Diego, and Honolulu. Serving many clients, Merit Protective Service uses polygraph methods to screen applicants for employment, employees seeking promotion, and personnel engaged in daily operations. Typical of its own work and that of many others in the field, it uses such slogans as "Employee dishonesty is the employer's responsibility" and "One dishonest employee can infect an entire organization."

California law protects those in the labor field from any possible injustice, for under the state's labor statutes, workers undergoing lie detector tests must first be shown the questions they are to be asked.

In support of the polygraph as a means of determining employee honesty, the Merit organization has this to say in its brochure:

Since the beginning of time man has sought the ideal means of interrogation. Ancient Indians would tie the suspect to poles and the first to succumb to the tortures would obviously be the guilty ones. Today, with the aid of the modern polygraph, lie detector, the art of interrogation has become a true science. It is a means to establish innocence as well as guilt. The lie detector is the sentinel of your security and a means of determining prior to employment the background and even the future plans of the prospective employee. Lie detector screening of employees on a planned basis eliminates almost all of the losses suffered by companies due to pilferage. With the proper indoctrination by our trained experts your employee will readily submit to these examinations.

Stephen Long, vice president of the Merit Corporation, who functions in the San Francisco office as its chief polygraphist, deals with domestic as well as industrial conflicts. He proudly tells of his success in using a polygraph to unite two sisters who for years had feuded bitterly over scandalous charges of immoral conduct made by one of them.

One of the women, fashionably dressed and personable, first called on Long to request an interview. "I'm frightfully distressed," she began, "and I've been told that perhaps you can help me with that instrument you call a lie detector."

"Give me the whole story," Long retorted. "I'm listening."

"You see," she said, pausing to open her handbag, take out a handkerchief, and dry her eyes, "it's like this. We're two sisters; I'm married, and my sister has always been single. Until this thing happened a year ago, we adored each other. We were inseparable; went everywhere together; shared our secrets; yes, we were really like one person. Never did two people love each other so dearly with trust and respect. And then it happened . . . ."

"What happened?" Long interrupted, trying to speed up the conversation.

"I'm coming to that," replied the visitor. "It was after I had arranged a trip abroad and my sister asked me if she could move into our house and live there with my husband—her brother-in-law—until I returned. Of course I agreed; there was no reason not to. But when I returned, I thought I had good reason to suspect that there had been an affair between my sister and my husband. I minced no words in telling her of my suspicions. She denied everything, as did my husband, and we've been enemies since. We live like people from two different worlds. We scream at each other, insult each other—there hasn't been a friendly word exchanged between us ever since."

"And just what do you want me to do about it?" Long inquired.

"Can't you give my sister a lie detector test and find out for sure if she is telling the truth when she denies improper relations with my husband?"

"That would be simple," Long replied, "but she would have to be willing. Under the circumstances I doubt if she would consent, and . . ."

"She'd agree to it in a minute," the caller interrupted. "I've proposed it to her, and it's the only suggestion I've ever made that she accepted."

"Then what's stopping us?" said Long. "The sooner the better. Bring your sister in. I'll explain to her what's involved, and if she's still agreeable, we'll make an appointment for the test."

A few days later Long received a call from the sister. The unmarried one readily consented to the examination, and an appointment was made.

Long started the examination with some preliminary interrogation on trivial matters. Then he went directly to the root of the problem. "Did you have an affair with Tom [not the husband's real name] during your sister's absence?" he asked. "Have you ever discussed this sort of thing with him?" and "Have you ever kissed Tom?"

The sister answered each question with an emphatic "No." At each negative response, the pens remained in constant, unchanged position, showing not the slightest tendency to even waver. It was undeniable proof, Long asserted, that the woman was telling the truth.

Her sister was then called into the room and told of the

results. In an instant, both women flew into each other's arms, kissed, and began to sob hysterically. Arm in arm, they walked out of the office, their faces beaming.

In a somewhat similar situation, Long reunited a couple that had separated after the wife charged her husband with infidelity.

"It took place in our Honolulu office," Long recalled. "In this situation the wife had accused her husband of unfaithfulness and had insisted he had a mistress. The man, vigorously denying the accusation, volunteered to undergo a lie detector test, and the wife readily agreeed to abide by the results.

"The examination supported the husband's claim of innocence, and the two kissed, and made up, and left together happily, so you can see that there's a valuable use for the lie detector besides trying to learn whether defendants and witnesses are telling the truth."

Long also explained how the technique was used to uncover pilfering in industrial concerns. He recalled a case in San Francisco, where a suspected employee of a national mercantile firm was believed to be stealing merchandise. The man emphatically denied his guilt. However, when given a lie detector test, he was shown to be untruthful. Faced with this conclusion, the man confessed his guilt, implicated others, and exposed a ring of thieving employees.

In a case in Buffalo, New York, a woman employed by a large department store was observed failing to record a sale of $1. Under constant questioning, she broke down and admitted having stolen $15,000 in cash. Her employers insisted that she undergo a lie detector . test, which resulted in the further admission that her prolonged thefts had totaled more than $52,000.

Because of his years of experience, Long has much to say in support of the accuracy of the lie detector when used by a competent operator. To this writer he said:

> There have been many opinions, comments, viewpoints, and statements in regard to polygraph examinations and the advantages or disadvantages of the giving of such tests. I believe that by viewing the use of the polygraph not only as a lie detection instrument but also as a truth verification instrument, it is easier to evaluate the advantageous pos-

sibilities of such an invention. The instrument itself is not mysterious and possesses no magical qualities. It is a scientifically designed instrument which measures several physical and psychological changes in the human body. It can be looked upon as an achievement similar to medical instruments which are used to observe and document physical phenomena.

I believe the conflicting opinions on the polygraph instrument and its uses should be concentrated not on the actual mechanism, but rather on those persons who administer examinations. Any functional instrument can be misused and its achievements proved minimal or useless. However, if used by a person competent and well trained, the instrument becomes a useful tool. Its potentials are realized and provide results otherwise not available.

Therefore, it is my opinion that we can shift offense or defense from the instrument to the person entrusted with its use.... I certainly do not condone results obtained by an unqualified examiner but feel that reasonable consideration should be given to persons who have taken the time and effort to study, investigate, research, and learn the art of polygraph examination. They are more qualified to debate the effectiveness, explain the uses, and set forth the accomplishments that can be obtained through the use of polygraph examination. These persons are also the fortunate witnesses of cases where polygraph examination has aided in proving the innocence of an accused person and separated fact from supposition. I feel the same consideration should be extended to trained and qualified examiners that is extended to trained experts in any field of endeavor.

In addition to the use of the lie detector in industrial and domestic situations, another lesser known application of the technique is to determine the truth in disputed paternity cases. This is clearly explained in an unusual paper written by John E. Reid, head of John E. Reid and Associates, based in Chicago, and Richard O. Arthur, top executive of the New York office of that establishment. They introduce the subject with an explanation that a paternity suit is usually initiated by a mother alleging that a certain man is the father of her child. She asks the court to have him legally declared the father so that he can be held responsible for the child's support.

The defendant, the writers point out, usually invokes one or two defenses. He may deny any sexual intercourse with the complainant during the possible period of the child's conception, or he may admit intercourse but claim the plaintiff also had sexual relations with other men during that time. In most cases, one or the other of the contestants will lie in trying to prove his or her position. The writers state:

> A court confronted with a paternity case may or may not have at its disposal the facilities for having blood-grouping tests of the complainant, the defendant, and the child. Even if the court does have access to blood-grouping tests, such tests can only exclude the defendant as being the child's father. They cannot prove that he is the father. The reason for this limitation is readily apparent when the basic principle of blood-grouping tests is understood. The basis for the tests is that a child inherits his particular blood group and blood types from one or both of his parents. For example, if the child is Group A, he must have inherited the A Group from either the mother or the father. If his mother is Group B, and the accused man is also Group B, the accused man could not possibly be the actual father. . . .
>
> For years a number of judges of the Chicago Municipal Court have consistently availed themselves of the lie detector technique to assist them in their decisions. Upon such occasions both the accused and the mother are requested by the judge to take a lie detector test. . . .
>
> On the basis of a six-year study of the 312 disputed paternity cases handled at the Chicago laboratory of John E. Reid and Associates, it was determined that 93 percent of the tested parties lied in some respect when they testified in court as to their sexual relationship.
>
> Although lie detector test results are ordinarily inadmissible in court as evidence, an exception to the rule is involved in these cases. This exception occurs when both parties agree and stipulate before any tests that the results of such tests are to be admitted in the trial as evidence, regardless of the tests' outcome. To request lie detector tests is often the defendant's only hope if he is to prove his contention that he did not have intercourse with the complainant during the baby's conception period. Rather than accuse the man who is the actual father, the mother often decides to accuse the man she loves as being the father of her child in the hope that he will marry

her. Or she accuses a single man or a man with money or a good job, rather than the man who is the father.

Without lie detector examinations, the judge or jury often are forced to come to a decision based more on intuition than facts and they can only hope that they are right. If they find in favor of the defendant and are wrong in this decision, an innocent child and mother will be harmed financially and forced to suffer further embarrassment. If they find in favor of the mother and are wrong, in this decision an innocent man is forced to pay a large sum of money and face an unfriendly wife, family, and friends because of his supposed indiscretion. These unfortunate consequences can be avoided almost entirely by the use of the highly reliable lie detector technique. . . .

12

When Experts Disagree

When two polygraphists disagree on the results of a lie detector examination, the trial judge may arbitrarily decide whose opinion to accept. This assumption of authority came as disheartening news to Joseph Arman Oliver, a 26-year-old maintenance man employed by a large department store in Kansas City, Missouri.

The fatal decision was made in the winter of 1972 while Oliver was on trial for abducting a girl of 18 from a street corner, driving her across the state line to Prairie Village, Kansas, and raping her there. The charge involved violation of a federal statute forbidding interstate transportation for immoral purposes.

The alleged victim was Jalaine McQuay, a student at the Atlantic Airlines School in Kansas City and a resident of a dormitory maintained for girls studying to become airline hostesses. Miss McQuay told the police that at 9:30 P.M. on November 16, 1972, she was walking alone to a nearby shopping center when she was accosted by a man she later identified as Oliver. He seized her forcefully, she said, carried her into his car, and drove across the state border into Kansas, Stopping at a lonely spot, he then dragged her from the car and raped her.

Freeing herself from her abductor after a violent struggle, Miss McQuay ran over a darkened road to a nearby house, telephoned the police, and gave officers a detailed description of her attacker. The next morning she was at police headquarters looking through mug shots of sex offenders known to be at large. Suddenly she stopped and called to an officer sitting close by.

"This is him," she exclaimed, handing over a photograph of Oliver, who, according to police records, had come to Kansas City in 1965 from Los Angeles, where he had been involved in sex-related offenses requiring occasional psychiatric treatment.

"Are you positive?" the officer inquired. "This is a pretty serious charge that you're making."

"I'd know him out of a thousand men," she retorted. "There's no question about it."

Several hours later Oliver was in custody, but his version of the episode differed from that of his accuser. He insisted he had picked up the girl on a street corner without difficulty and that she had entered his car willingly. He also admitted having had sexual intercourse with her, but again he asserted that she was a willing partner. He even added that after their tryst she had demanded $20 from him and had become incensed when he refused to pay.

"There was nothing like rape involved in this affair," he told the police. "This girl had no objection to what was going on."

When his accuser later denied this explanation, police called the FBI, which took over the case and booked Oliver for a violation of federal law. The case finally reached the federal grand jury, which listened to the girl's story and corroborating police statements before voting an indictment against Oliver.

The trial opened on the morning of December 15, 1972, before Judge William H. Becker of the U.S. Court for the Western District of Missouri. Oliver, who had entered a plea of not guilty, had previously insisted on a lie detector test. His attorney had agreed to the test, and Virgil L. Hollis, a polygraphist from Prairie Village, was called on to conduct the examination. On its completion, Hollis reported that in his judgment Oliver had spoken the truth when he denied forcing the girl into the car or threatening her.

Hollis' findings, however, were not admitted as evidence in the trial, and on April 16, Oliver was found guilty by a jury and sentenced to twenty years in prison.

Oliver's attorney immediately appealed to the Court of Appeals of the Eighth District, which reversed the conviction and ordered a retrial. The appeal was based largely on the defense claim that the trial court had erred in refusing to permit the victim's roommates to testify as to Miss McQuay's reputation for truthfulness, her veracity having been questioned by the defense.

With the possibility of a second trial, Oliver demanded a second lie detector test. He was confident that its results would support those of Hollis' examination. A stipulation was entered into by opposing counsel, whereby it was agreed that the results of a second examination would be admitted into evidence, regardless of which side they favored.

Judge Becker, accepting the stipulation, wanted to be absolutely sure that Oliver understood the meaning of this agreement and accepted its terms willingly. For this reason the defendant was carefully examined by the court as the following dialogue between judge and defendant illustrates:

The Court: The first question is whether you are willing to agree that the results of the polygraph test are subject to being introduced in evidence by the government if they are unfavorable to you. You are not required to make any such agreement.

Oliver: Right from the beginning I have always wanted to take another polygraph test, and that holds true now, regardless of the consequences, regardless of how the court wants to use the results.

The Court: What you are being asked now is whether you are willing that the government be permitted to use the results if they are unfavorable you?

Oliver: Right. I say yes. I agree to that.

The Court: You understand that no one can require you to make this agreement, don't you?

Oliver: Yes, your Honor.

The Court: And this is an intelligent, understanding, and voluntary agreement that you are proposing to make?

Oliver: Yes.

The Court: Are you willing to answer the questions propounded by the examiner and furnish him the information he needs, knowing that you cannot be required to do so?

Oliver: Yes, your Honor.

The Court: And you know that if the results are unfavorable, they may be used against you by the government?

Oliver: Yes, sir.

With this colloquy between judge and defendant concluded to the full satisfaction of both, the defense considered the selection of a second polygraphist. It was finally decided to engage Leonard H. Harrelson of Chicago. Government counsel approved the selection.

On September 8, 1974, Harrelson arrived in Kansas City and performed a lie detector examination of the accused. Much to Oliver's dismay Harrelson reported that he had found Oliver's answers deceptive, especially his response to such questions as: "Did the girl tell the truth about what happened?"; "Did the girl get into your car willingly?"; and "Did you threaten her?"

However, Harrelson admitted that in his judgment Oliver had been truthful in responding to the following question: "Did you engage in sexual intercourse with the girl?" And he emphasized his conclusion that Oliver had told the truth when answering affirmatively this query: "Did she want to have sex with you?"

Judge Becker and opposing counsel were advised of Harrelson's conclusions, but the unexpected upset did not come until Oliver's second trial was well under way.

Obviously, the defense had intended to make much of the disagreement between the two polygraphists, using it to weaken Harrelson's testimony, but Judge Becker had other ideas. He readily allowed the Chicago expert to testify; but to the dismay of the defense, the court ruled that Hollis would not be permitted to take the stand and reveal his contrary opinions. Explaining his ruling, Judge Becker declared that in his judgment Hollis was not a qualified polygraph expert.

Two days later the jury found Oliver guilty. He was sentenced to a life term in federal prison, a far more severe punishment than he would have suffered under the first sentence. Ironically, fate was also cruel to Hollis, who was murdered in August 1976.

Oliver and his counsel were angered by the final results of the second trial, and an appeal was filed with the U.S. Court of Appeals. Its main contentions were that the court had erred in excluding Hollis' testimony and in denying the request that the girl's roommates be permitted to testify as to her reputation for truthfulness. There were other issues as well, based on technicalities.

The high court's ruling, handed down on October 31, 1975, marked still further defeat for Oliver, for the justices affirmed the conviction. The appellate justices gave short shrift to the defendant's claim that the stipulation and agreement on the second lie detector test were "in violation of his rights." His dialogue with the court on this issue was cited.

The chief disagreement enumerated in the appeal was Judge Becker's refusal to permit Hollis to testify and the court's allowance of Harrelson's findings in evidence. Said the court:

> This appeal necessarily raises the issue whether the state of the art of polygraph examinations had advanced to a level of reliability sufficient to make the tests admissible in evidence. Judicial opinions pertaining to admission of polygraph testimony seem all to point to exclusion.... Despite the almost uniform exclusion of such evidence, this court has recognized that 'recent decisions have found under certain circumstances a polygraph examination may be admissible.'

Referring to the appellant's argument that Judge Becker's refusal to admit Hollis' favorable testimony was in error, the justices concluded:

> Defendant also asserts that the trial court abused its discretion in excluding the testimony of Mr. Hollis. His testimony took on increased importance to the defense following Oliver's failure of the polygraph examination given by Mr. Harrelson. The District Court, however, rejected any testimony by Mr. Hollis for two fundamental reasons. First, it ruled that he did not appear to have the requisite qualifications of a polygraph expert. Second, his test was found unreliable because of his lack of expertise and the limitations placed upon his administration of the examination by the defense.
>
> The record discloses that the qualifications of Mr. Hollis are minimal, especially when compared to those of Mr. Harrelson. Expert testimony concerning polygraph results demands more than minimal qualifications.... Under the circumstances we fail to find the exclusion of his testimony to be an abuse of the trial court's discretion.

In this respect the Appellate Court supported its opinion by reference to the judgment of Herbert Briick, an FBI agent who was present during the last examination. Briick, said to be experienced in polygraphy, corroborated Harrelson's conclusion and approved the technique he had used. In conclusion, the justices said:

> The record fails to sustain the claim of bias on the part of Mr. Harrelson.
>
> Furthermore, it should be emphasized that the qualifications and expertise of Mr. Harrelson are of the highest order. In fact, he was initially selected by the defendant.

The defense, still dissatisfied, carried a further appeal to the U.S. Supreme Court, which refused to review the case.

A Priest Turns
Polygraphist

U nlike Vollmer, Keeler, and Reid, not all distinguished lie detector experts began their careers as policemen or crime laboratory technicians. One of them was a Catholic priest.

He was the late Father Walter G. Summers S.J., a noted psychologist at Fordham University in New York. Father Summers died September 24, 1938, at the height of a brilliant career. A native New Yorker, he was widely known as the inventor of a new type of polygraph, technically called a psychogalvanometer or pathometer, which registers the variation in the minute electrical currents coursing through the body. For his personally designed apparatus he claimed 100 percent accuracy. In March 1938, his testimony was admitted in a New York court, the first time such evidence was allowed there. It resulted in vindication and freedom for a man convicted of robbery.

For his role in this case Father Summers gained nationwide acclaim. Testifying about the results of his lie detector test on the defendant Raymond Kenny in Queens County Court, he set an important legal precedent of national significance. "It was the first time that the results of a stipulated lie detector test have ever been introduced in evidence, so far as I know, in this state or any other jurisdiction," said Kenny's attorney, Paul O'Dwyer, now president of the Council of the City of New York.

Father Summers, born March 23, 1889, the son of John and Mary Summers, was an eager seeker of knowledge in many fields, but psychology held his greatest interest.

After attending the High School of Commerce, he entered St. Francis Xavier College and later Woodstock College, where he was awarded a B.A. degree. He subsequently earned his Ph.D. at Georgetown University and a similar honor came from a college in Rome. He joined the Jesuit Order on August 14, 1917, and was ordained at Georgetown four years later.

He served as professor of physics at Georgetown from 1914 to 1919 and was given a chair as professor of psychology, which he held from 1923 to 1930. In 1931 he resigned this post to accept a similar position at Fordham's Graduate School, a post he occupied until his sudden death from coronary thrombosis. He was the author of many textbooks.

During his important and busy years at Fordham, Father Summers traveled extensively, visiting centers of psychology in Paris, Berlin, Prague, and Rome. In Vienna he studied for a time and lectured on his favorite subject before many important gatherings of scholars.

The *Fordham Ram*, a student publication, reported his death in a touching eulogy on September 30, 1938:

> At Fordham, Father Summers will be remembered for his almost miraculous organization of the psychology course, which, under his tutelage, grew from four to one hundred and ten students in almost five years. . . . The child clinic which started at St. Vincent's Hospital, was under the personal direction of Father Summers. The service of this clinic was to observe children of all types and to assist by this observation in the solving of child problems. Dr. Leon Goldrich, the late director of child guidance in the City of New York, said that the guidance bureau at Fordham was the best integrated he had ever seen. . . .
>
> Perhaps Father Summers' greatest bid to fame was his 'lie detector.' This machine was the product of his combined proficiency in psychology, physics, and the sciences. The machine, called a pathometer, recorded the electrical changes that accompany emotional disturbances and in this fashion

revealed whether a person was speaking the truth or not. Father Summers maintained that the technique was the most important in the use of this detector. Unless the questions were judiciously selected, properly spaced, and well arranged, and unless the charts were properly interpreted, the recording would suffer accordingly.

The detector was known the world over and had been employed in several criminal cases. Because of its outstanding success in these cases, the lie detector had become part of the equipment of the Rhode Island State Police and Bureau of Criminal Investigation of New York. Only recently Father Summers had read a paper on his invention before the International Association of Chiefs of Police at Toronto. The detector was also on exhibition at the Syracuse State Fair.

At the time of his death, the beloved priest was compiling notes for a new book that would tell of his latest research into the subject of brain waves and emotional reactions. Just what inspired the priest to become so deeply interested in the lie detector and in techniques pertaining to its use is not recorded, but it is presumed that as a psychologist he was deeply concerned with the quest for truth and how to obtain it in difficult situations.

Many of his ideas on the subject are explained in his article, "Science Can Get the Confession." published in Fordham's *Law Review*. It is an essay replete with succinct comments on the subject that deserve repetition here. They include:

Lie detector tests may be used to establish the innocence of an accused person. Such a test may also be requested by a person accused or suspected of the commission of a crime. In our work with the lie detector, the test has established the innocence of the accused almost as often as it has established the guilt of the suspect. . . .

If a person not merely consents to a deception test but requests that he be permitted to undergo such an examination, no phase of self-incrimination is involved, and the admissibility of the evidence would depend largely on the validy of the test suggested or implied. . . .

Although there is weight of evidence on the legal side against the admission of lie detection tests, we cannot escape the weight of authority for the admissibility of well-established and scientific tests. A review of the legal literature on this topic clearly shows that the entire discussion has centered about the admissibility of blood pressure tests of deception. . . .

We believe that a procedure which starts out with an experimental validity of 85 percent is an extremely hazardous thing to employ in the investigation of the guilt or innocence of any person. . . .

For the past five years we have been experimenting at Fordham University with various psychogalvanometric procedures with the object of developing a method for the more exact measurement of emotion. We gradually developed a technique which not only proved valuable for the measurement of the concomitants of emotional reaction, but which enabled us to verify the accuracy of the introspective reports of subjects. . . .

These criteria were subjected to a most critical evaluation in a test of fifty groups of persons which involved 271 individuals. The selection was one which approximated in all details the conditions of a criminal investigation. Our preliminary tests showed an efficiency of better than 99 percent. The critical test was intended to evaluate our technique and procedure in the discrimination of the guilty, accomplices, and the innocent. In this critical test our procedure showed an efficiency of 98-plus percent. . . .

Father Summers had already earned wide recognition in the psychology fields when he was called on to assist in the defense of Raymond Kenny, who had been arrested for the holdup of a market in Queens County, New York, on July 12, 1937. Although Kenny denied any part in the crime, the police thought they had a strong case against him, especially since Kenny was a second offender under a similar charge.

Kenny engaged Paul O'Dwyer to defend him, but despite a strong defense, the accused man was found guilty in October of that year. O'Dwyer immediately filed an appeal on the grounds of newly discovered evidence and was successful in winning a new trial. Judge Golden, who wrote the appeals court decision, commented: "I am of the opinion that in the interest of justice there should be a reexamination of all the facts in this case before another jury."

Anticipating the second legal contest, O'Dwyer enlisted the services of Father Summers, asking the priest to test the accused with the specially designed pathometer.

With court permission, Kenny was taken under guard to Fordham University, where he was examined by the priest. Afterwards, Father Summers told O'Dwyer that he believed the prisoner was telling the truth in denying his guilt. O'Dwyer was gratified, but doubted whether these findings could be admitted in evidence at the second trial. Nevertheless, he determined to try.

At the outset, the judge was dubious. First, he said, he must satisfy himself of the celebrated priest's qualifications. With the jury excluded, Father Summers took the stand. To justify his belief in the accuracy of his new lie detector, he testified that his study of the instrument and its use had covered more than six thousand individual tests. He continued with a long explanation of the scientific principles involved, an exposition which no doubt convinced the court of the psychologist's ability. After he had concluded, the judge announced that Father Summers would be accepted as a witness and that his testimony would be admitted in evidence.

After the jury had returned to the box, the priest, over the objections of the prosecution, repeated all that he had previously stated, ending with his conclusions as to the defendant's truthfulness. After hearing several other witnesses, the jury retired. Its deliberations extended through the entire night and into the early morning.

The hands of the courtroom clock stood at exactly 2:30 on the morning of March 30 when the jury returned to the courtroom and announced its verdict: Not guilty.

The verdict was angrily received by the prosecution, which still insisted that Father Summers' testimony should not have been admitted in evidence. Accordingly, it appealed to the higher court, which on March 29, 1938, rendered its historic decision sustaining Kenny's acquittal.

In its decision the court emphasized the convincing strength of Father Summers' testimony and explained why it believed its admission was legal and proper. Said the high court in part:

Decision on the question now before the court should be
approached with the same breadth of vision which character-
izes the decision made by Mr. Justice Steinbrink wherein that
distinguished jurist says: 'Law and jurisprudence, which are
something more than the dry tomes of the past, can be
understood by considering fundamental principles not only of
government and economics but also at times by giving
consideration in particular cases to sociology, medicine, or
other sciences, philosophy, and history. New concepts must
beat down the crystalized resistance of the legally trained
mind that always seeks precedent before the new is accepted
into law. Frequently we must look ahead and not back-
wards. . . .'

Objection to scientific proof is not at all novel. At one time
or another in their development, testimony as to fingerprints,
as to X-rays, as to handwriting, as to bullet markings, and as to
psychiatric examinations were all refused admission into
evidence. . . . Their gradual admission into evidence came only
after many rebuffs and rejections at the hands of various
courts. Today their right to admission in evidence is firmly
entrenched in our law. . . .

For hundreds of years our courts have deemed the examination and cross-examination of witnesses in open court to be
the best method so far devised for the ascertainment of the
truth and have used that method for lack of any better
approach. It seems to me that this pathometer and the
technique by which it is used indicate a new and more
scientific approach to the ascertainment of truth in legal
investigations. The objection of the district attorney to the
admission of the testimony in question is overruled.

O'Dwyer's overwhelming legal victory had a strange and
disappointing sequel. Flushed with success, he tried his utmost
to introduce Father Summers' testimony and technique in a
somewhat similar case in Kings County a short time later. "It
was not possible," he later wrote. "I could not even get the
machine into the jail to make the test and I tried to set aside the
conviction on that ground, but it failed, the court having
concluded that the test was not scientifically accepted."

How Binding Are Confessions?

S upporters of the lie detector often argue that when polygraph tests disclose untruthfulness they often lead to confessions, thus saving the state the cost of long trials and putting a stamp of certainty on the administration of justice. In two memorable cases, one in Ohio and the other in Oregon, adverse lie detector tests led to confessions and convictions which were affirmed on appeal. In both cases the admissibility of the confessions became the subject of bitter courtroom controversies, and the opinions of the trial judges surprised participating lawyers.

In 1964, Charles E. McDevitt, a branch manager for the National Bank of Toledo, Ohio, was indicted on charges of embezzling more than $2,500 in small amounts from his employers. The defalcations had come to light when examiners audited the bank's books and discovered a shortage.

Prior to the trial, George Kerwin, a polygraphist in private practice, gave McDevitt a lie detector test.

After this examination, Kerwin told bank officials that he had discovered definite evidence of deception. The bankers then plied McDevitt with specific and pointed questions which he readily answered in detail, this time fully admitting his guilt. In fact, he confessed that he had converted bank funds to his own use and signed a statement to that effect. He spared no details.

Pressed for an explanation of his methods, he shamefacedly named certain tellers, and said he had juggled their accounts to cover his embezzlement. The largest single amount he admitted taking was $750.

McDevitt was then brought to trial, but to the surprise of those in the crowded courtroom he pleaded not guilty. When asked why he was pleading not guilty after willingly signing a confession, he replied: "Because our training as branch managers is that the branch manager has the responsibility of anything that goes on at the branch."

While the government had planned to call Kerwin as a witness to testify against McDevitt, the court, after excusing the jury from the courtroom, ruled that no reference should be made to the specific results of the lie detector test itself. This ruling, however, did not apply to McDevitt's confession to the bank officials which was given after and as a result of the polygraph examination.

The jury found McDevitt guilty and he was sentenced to a year in prison. McDevitt then filed an appeal with the appellate court, contending that the confession was inadmissible because it followed the incriminating results of the lie detector test. The Appellate Court, in its final decision, affirmed the judgment of the trial court, stating:

> The trial court therefore was correct in holding that the voluntary confession signed by appellant was not rendered inadmissible by the fact that this confession was made following the polygraph test.
>
> Appellant next contends that there was not sufficient evidence to corroborate the confession . . . appellant confessed the details as to each conversion, setting forth the name of each teller from whose cage money was embezzled. Each of these tellers testified as witnesses, and the amounts of the shortages are supported by their testimony and their daily balance sheets for the dates in question. This evidence sufficiently corroborates the confession. We find that this evidence, together with the confession, supports the verdict of the jury.

The judgment of the District Court is affirmed.

In Oregon, Brian Lee Clifton suffered a fate similar to Charles McDevitt's. Convicted of killing the manager of a Portland motel, he appealed on the ground that the trial court had erred in receiving his confession as evidence because it was not given voluntarily.

Clifton's appeal was based largely on the contention that he was fatigued after an unsuccessful polygraph test and that his admission of guilt was influenced by his mental condition after the test.

Affirming the action of the trial court, the Supreme Court made this comment:

> At the beginning of the trial defendant moved to suppress the offer in evidence of his oral and written confessions. A hearing was then held at which testimony was received by the trial court as required by our decision in *State v. Brewton*.
>
> It appears from the testimony offered at that hearing that after defendant's arrest and after being informed of his constitutional rights he was then interrogated by the police for about two hours. He then agreed to submit to a polygraph examination. According to defendant, he was at that time extremely fatigued from lack of food and sleep during the period prior to his arrest and asked for a lawyer several times during that interrogation.
>
> Upon the completion of the polygraph examination, defendant was told by the officers that it showed he was 'deceptive.' According to defendant, he was also told by the police repeatedly that he might have 'done it' because he 'liked to kill' or for several reasons; that this is what his mother might think when she 'found out,' that defendant became angry at the continued reference to sexual conduct. Much of defendant's testimony was denied by the police officers.
>
> In any event, defendant broke down and cried and confessed to the killing, saying that he went to rob the motel and killed an innocent person. A detailed confession was then 'taped' and also transcribed and signed.
>
> At the conclusion of the hearing the trial court denied defendant's motion to suppress. The court then entered 'special findings' that defendant had been effectively advised

of all of his constitutional rights; that he therefore knowingly waived such rights; that his confessions were 'freely and voluntarily made and were not the product of any promises, threats, duress, or coercion of any nature whatsover'; and that 'the procedures used in conducting the polygraph examination were fair and reasonable and did not constitute . . . a coercion process.

Despite these findings of fact by the trial court, defendant contends that 'the psychological coercion' resulting from the use of the polygraph examination prevented defendant from fairly exercising his constitutional right to remain silent.

In support of that position defendant contends that the polygraph, as used in this case, was coercive because defendant who 'believed' in the polygraph, was told that he had been found by the polygraph to be deceptive, despite the fact that polygraphs are not completely reliable. Defendant also complains that he was extremely fatigued at the time of the polygraph test and that it was an improper examination; that this may affect its accuracy; and that it was improper for the police to suggest that he might have killed because he 'liked to kill' or for sexual reasons.

This case does not involve the offer of polygraph evidence at the trial before a jury of a criminal case. . . . Instead, this case involves the sufficiency of the evidence offered in a preliminary hearing before the trial court to establish that a confession was given voluntarily so as to be admissible in evidence at such a trial.

Defendant testified at the hearing that he was told that 'according to the examination' he had been 'very deceptive' and had been 'lying.' This was apparently true. We recognize . . . that the polygraph has not yet attained general scientific acceptance as a reliable and accurate means of ascertaining truth or deception. For that reason the results of polygraph examinations are held by most courts to be inadmissible as substantive evidence on the issue of the guilt or innocence of a criminal case.

To the surprise of many lawyers following the case, the high court took advantage of the opportunity to record its approval of the use of the lie detector by the police—a move unusual in most court decisions in which judges describe the polygraph as inaccurate and unreliable.

In its conclusion, the court volunteered this opinion of the machine:

> Nevertheless, we believe that the polygraph is a proper tool for use by the police in interrogating persons suspected of a crime, provided that such persons agree to voluntarily submit to such examinations and that such examinations are properly conducted. To hold otherwise and to hold that upon completion of such a polygraph examination the police may not inform the person who has taken the examination that it appears from the polygraph that he has been deceptive would, as a practical matter, foreclose the effectiveness of the polygraph examination by the police in the investigation of crime . . . .

> Upon the question whether defendant's subsequent confession was voluntary, however, we believe that such a fact was not sufficient, either alone or when considered together with the other facts in this case, to render defendant's confession involuntary as a matter of law.

> The trial judge, after hearing the testimony offered by both parties at the hearing on defendant's motion to suppress the confession, some of which was conflicting, found that defendant's confession was given voluntarily. After examining the record we find there was substantial evidence to support that finding. Affirmed.

How the Polygraph
Can Help

The loud ringing of the telephone broke the quiet of the sheriff's office in Martinez, the county seat of Contra Costa County in California. It was the night of December 21, 1974. Picking up the receiver, the deputy on duty listened to the excited voice of a man, obviously eager to report important information.

"Never mind who I am," the caller began. " Better get some men out here. There's a body on the highway."

"Where's 'out here'?" inquired the officer.

"On the Port Chicago highway near the town of Nichols."

"There'll be men on the way in a minute or two," the caller was told. "Wait there so they'll know just where to look."

Minutes later a sheriff's car filled with deputies was on its way. Approaching the scene, the deputies observed a lone man pointing to a body lying beside the highway.

"There he is," called out the stranger, who later explained that he was driving alone in his car when he observed the corpse.

Minutes later one of the deputies was scrambling for a telephone to notify Harry D. Ramsay, sheriff and coroner of the county. Awaiting his arrival, the officers made only a cursory examination of the remains. They found that the victim had been about 20 years old and that he had been stabbed several times in the upper part of the body. Search of the scene for the murder weapon was futile.

Later, Dr. William Bogart, the county medical officer, conducted a postmortem examination and found seven wounds caused by a knife blade fully six and a half inches long.

The identity of the victim remained a mystery while deputies busied themselves checking fingerprints and looking at missing person reports.

Two days passed before fingerprints revealed that the dead man had been William Patsel, Jr., of whom practically nothing was known. It became apparent that a hunt for the slayer would depend largely on what the sheriff's investigators could learn about Patsel. With no clue on which to work, they set out to discover Patsel's occupation and the motive for his murder. Days of intensive inquiry followed until it was learned that Patsel, an unemployed clerk, had been an acquaintance of one Charles Crowell, whose address they had been given.

Hurrying to Crowell's home, the deputies observed a car parked by the curb and were told that it belonged to Crowell. It was a two-door Chevrolet, and a close examination of the vehicle revealed blood stains on the rear passenger seat and a red-stained palm print on the outside surface.

A ring of the bell of a nearby apartment house brought Crowell to the door, and he appeared to be surprised by the presence of uniformed men. Asked what he knew of Patsel and the murder, he admitted knowing the deceased as "Bill" but insisted he had no knowledge of the killing.

Crowell reluctantly accompanied the officers to headquarters, where it was established that the bloody palm print was identical to one taken of the suspect at the police identification bureau.

Sheriff Ramsay immediately took charge of Crowell's interrogation but to little avail. The suspect, with an air of bravado, insisted he had nothing to reveal. "I've got nothing to tell you," he declared, "because really I don't know nothing."

"Well, then," the sheriff demanded, "tell me when this man Patsel was in your car and where you went with him?"

Crowell in answer merely shrugged his shoulders. "I'm telling you I don't remember," he replied with a show of defiance.

"If that's the way you intend to cooperate," Sheriff Ramsay

retorted, "I think you should take a lie detector test. If you really know nothing about this murder, as you say, the polygraph will tell us whether you're telling the truth."

"I'm ready; let's go," said Crowell, and soon he and the sheriff were on their way to the office of the county polygraphist, Detective Sergeant Herman B. Roller, an experienced technician who still teaches the art and other subjects related to criminology in the county's public schools.

Roller's task proved to be difficult and aggravating. It was apparent that Crowell was determined not to talk or to reveal any information that might help the authorities.

"I told you I don't know nothin' about this," Crowell repeated over and over. It was all that he would say, but Roller had encountered such types before and knew how to handle them.

One question followed another with the same results. Two hours passed, with Crowell still maintaining his sullen silence.

"I can't make you talk," the exasperated polygraphist exclaimed, "but I'm telling you this. It will be decidedly to your advantage to tell me what you know. You must realize that you're really in a tough spot."

Crowell began to squirm in his chair, and Roller realized that the man's nerves were beginning to break. There was perspiration on his face.

"Just what the hell do you want to know?" Crowell finally asked.

"Who was with you in the car last night? And what time did you get home?"

"There were three of us, if you must know. We'd been drinking heavily, and all of us were pretty drunk. One of them was the man who's dead; I guess you know by now that his name was Patsel. We were driving him home. Patsel was in the back seat, The third man was in the front seat beside me. I was driving. Somehow Patsel and the man sitting with me got into some sort of a stupid drunken argument, and the guy with me jumped over to the back seat and let Patsel have it—a blow on the head and a knife several times in the back. Pretty soon Patsel was dead."

"What's the name of the man who did the stabbing?" Roller demanded.

In an instant, Crowell's manner changed. "I'm no stool," he shot back angrily.

During all of this dialogue Roller's eyes were on the polygraph paper and he was satisfied Crowell was telling the truth. He was, however, determined to learn the name of the man who had done the stabbing. Pressing hard, he finally induced Crowell to tell.

"If you must know," said Crowell, speaking reluctantly, "his name is Emery Phillips. He's a laborer, but he's out of a job. He lives with me in my apartment."

"So you and this man Phillips disposed of the body," Roller prodded.

"What do you think?" Crowell retorted. "We couldn't go on driving with a dead man in the car, so we got ourselves to the highway and dumped Patsel there—just where you found him— then Phillips and I went home together and got to bed."

Crowell admitted having helped to lift the body from the car.

With the murderer now identified, the officers were convinced the mystery was solved, but they still wanted corroboration of Crowell's statements. A second polygraphist, Inspector George Marmon of Berkeley, was called on to examine Crowell a second time. The results were the same.

Meanwhile, officers had placed Phillips under arrest despite his pleas of innocence and his charge that Crowell had been lying. Charged with murder, Phillips sent for a lawyer, William Gagen, and told newsmen that he would have no difficulty in proving his innocence.

The trial was set for July 14, 1975, and Deputy District Attorney Michael Coleman, recognized as one of the ablest prosecutors in the county, was assigned to represent the state.

Two days were consumed in selecting a jury, and the trial proceeded with Crowell as the prosecution's star witness. Because the tests had not been stipulated, Crowell's accusing statements during the lie detector tests could not be introduced as evidence and the jurors found themselves unable to agree on a verdict.

The question of a second trial was seriously considered by

Coleman and his associates. They were dubious of such a course, for without the lie detector evidence they again would be obliged to depend largely on Crowell's testimony, which had been seriously weakened by Coleman's cross-examination.

The issue was still under discussion when Phillips announced his willingness to plead guilty to a felony charge of being an accessory to the murder. The plea was accepted by the court, which showed leniency by granting the defendant three years of probation, provided he would agree to serve some of this time in a halfway house for treatment of his alcoholism.

There were some who believed the sentence had been too lenient, but all agreed that without the lie detector the case would have remained an unsolved mystery.

Chasing A Spy

For more than four years the shrewdest agents in American and allied military intelligence carried on a top secret investigation on two continents. The investigation focused on Frank Hirt, a man suspected of being a Nazi spy, who later proved to be operating under direct orders from the Reich.

This exciting cloak-and-dagger mystery ended suddenly in the polygraph room of the Berkeley Police Department, when a lie detector expert unmasked the man and obtained an amazing confession.

Credit for this little-known achievement goes to a retired Berkeley police lieutenant, Albert E. Riedel. Considered by many to be the cleverest polygraph operator in the world, Riedel had used the lie detector to solve many murder cases and other baffling crimes.

A native-born American, Frank Hirt spent much of his life in Germany. He eventually became a soldier in the United States Air Force and might have succeeded in continuing his espionage if not for the results of a lie detector test.

The long and frustrating inquiry into Hirt's activities began before the United States entered World War II. British intelligence officers first became suspicious of his movements and shadowed him when he left Germany and began wandering through Switzerland.

After the United States entered the war against Germany and Japan following the attack on Pearl Harbor, American intelligence agents joined their British colleagues in keeping a watchful eye on Hirt, but they lacked direct or substantive evidence against him.

British intelligence men trailed Hirt to Bermuda where they became convinced that their suspicions were well founded. It was there that they observed Hirt flashing large rolls of American currency and spending lavishly. The British secretly examined Hirt's baggage and found documents revealing that he had once been arrested in Germany on suspicion of disloyalty and had been grilled by the military although he held the rank of corporal in Hitler's army.

Winning his confidence, the British investigators subtly asked Hirt how he came to possess so much American money. He was quick to explain that his German grandmother, fearing that he might some day be ordered to leave the Reich because of his American citizenship, had deliberately hoarded United States currency for him to use when he left the country. The British investigators also learned of his plans to fly to America aboard a plane that would land in Miami.

Upon Hirt's arrival there, FBI agents were on hand to pick up his trail. They followed him through many states until they learned that he had been drafted for service in the United States Air Force.

A skilled mechanic, Hirt was soon put to work on military bases and promoted to the rank of staff sergeant. Stubborn and cocky, he was disliked by associates and superiors alike. They often spoke of him as "a hot number" and he was transferred from one base to another. His constant movement added to the difficulties of investigators trying to keep pace with him.

Months of frustrating and secret investigation passed before intelligence officers met to decide what further action should be taken.

"Arrest him," a high officer said.

"And then what?" another inquired.

"He should be given a lie detector test," someone proposed, and the question turned to whether such an examination should take place in the East or West. Much discussion followed. It ended with a proposal from a major with a specific suggestion. "First he must be taken into custody," the officer said. "Then he should be taken to California for an examination by a police officer in the city of Berkeley, a man named Riedel, who is regarded as one of the cleverest polygraphists in America. The secret of his success, I'm told, is the way he frames his questions, and he has gotten confessions in cases that seemed beyond solution. Let's try him."

The proposal met with general approval, and after arrangements had been made with Riedel's superiors, Hirt was jailed and told that he would be moved under guard to Berkeley.

Several days later a taciturn Hirt arrived at Berkeley Police Headquarters under heavy guard and was led to the polygraph room. Riedel stood ready to undertake his military assignment. He realized that he would be confronting one of the most difficult and important challenges in his long career.

First Riedel showed Hirt the detector itself and explained how the apparatus worked. Then he adjusted the belt around his subject's waist and tightened the blood pressure arm cuff. Hirt feigned interest and asked many questions, but his attitude was belligerent and he asserted that the test would bring about full vindication.

"Is this contraption absolutely accurate?" he inquired at one point.

"Absolutely so," Riedel replied confidently. "You can't fool it no matter how hard you try. If you lie to me, I'll know it in an instant."

"That's what you think," Hirt retorted.

Questioning began with Riedel slowly leading into the man's status and his purpose in the United States. Hirt shot back quick answers with a smirk on his face, but his confident manner didn't fool the polygraph.

"It won't help you any to lie," Riedel said. "This instrument tells me you're lying." In the back of the examiner's mind was the hope that proper strategy might lead to a confession.

"Are you a Nazi, and are you snooping in this country for Hitler?" Riedel finally demanded in an exasperated tone. "Come clean and tell me the truth. This instrument says that you've been lying."

"No," came the decisive answer, but again the polygraph pens swerved far from their original course.

"Another lie," said the examiner. "Don't you see, you just can't get away with it?"

Hirt's face suddenly blanched. "Hell," he exclaimed in an exasperated voice. "I see I can't get away with it. I might as well tell you the truth. Now listen . . . "

The story that the man slowly unfolded—a full confession—was startling. Not only did he frankly admit to spying for the Reich, but he also revealed every detail of his travels and his work under direct orders from Germany.

Recalling this experience years afterward, Riedel said that Hirt's admissions were so amazing that at times the polygraphist wondered whether he was being "taken." It was only after some of Hirt's revelations were found to coincide with essential details which had been given in advance by the military to Riedel, that the polygraphist realized he was listening to a true account.

Hirt began his long confession by explaining that as a native American he had been taken to Germany at the age of four. He remained there in the home of wealthy grandparents until he was 20, at which time he returned to American soil. Soon after that he went back to Germany, joined the Nazi Party, and became a corporal in Hitler's forces. Then he was told that he was destined to become a German spy and would be required to operate in the United States and Europe. He received technical aircraft training and was sent to a Berlin school directed by Karl Bauer, a notorious master spy whose responsibility was to train Nazis for foreign espionage.

Hirt admitted that the Gestapo had once become suspicious of his loyalty but claimed that he had finally convinced those in high places of his devotion to the Reich. His mission as a spy was to gather technical information about newly made American war planes, especially high-altitude bombers.

Hirt went on to explain that despite a degree of harassment by the Gestapo, who for reasons of their own questioned his faithfulness to the Party, he had succeeded in convincing the German intelligence authorities that he could be trusted to do what they wanted and was soon on his way to Switzerland. Before leaving Germany, however, he had been given the names and addresses of spy leaders in various cities of Europe and Latin America to whom he was to report for specific instructions.

"How did you communicate with them?" Riedel demanded.

Hirt laughed before boastfully relating how the Germans had given him a bottle of colorless liquid, actually invisible ink, and taught him to write with it using a toothpick wrapped in cotton for a pen. He said he would write a meaningless letter over the invisible one and that the original and secret message became visible only after the paper was dipped in a specially prepared chemical.

After the details of Hirt's confession had been put on paper, he was returned to military custody and confined in an American military prison. He remained there until long after the Nazi empire had collapsed. A trial was considered after the war, but high military authorities realized it would be useless to attempt a formal trial because the principal corroborating witnesses were either dead in Germany or in prison as war criminals. Hirt was finally returned to Germany, and he quickly vanished.

17

Mission to Guam

Former police associates of Lieutenant Albert Riedel assert that no account of his remarkable career would be complete without recalling his success in solving the baffling rape and murder of an attractive young woman on the island of Guam.

The crime took place on the night of December 11, 1948. The victim was 23-year-old Ruth Farnsworth, a former San Franciscan and onetime WAC, who had come to the island two years earlier to work as a Navy civil service employee. She was known as "the most beautiful girl on Guam." A deeply religious Mormon, she worked part-time in a jade shop and used her extra earnings to help support a brother then on a religious mission in Mexico.

When Ruth Farnsworth failed to return home on the fatal night, worried friends looked for her at the jade shop. They found it unoccupied and in total darkness, the electric wiring having been ripped away. Foul play had obviously occurred.

Lieutenant Commander James T. Hackett, the assistant police chief, was notified and immediately launched a widespread search. Enlisted men joined police in combing the island, but no clues were found. Thirty-seven hours of intensive work passed before searchers discovered the young woman lying unconscious in a jungle near the shop where she worked. She had been brutally beaten, strangled, and raped. Heroic measures by doctors in an island hospital were to no avail, and she died eighteen hours later. Her fiance, Marine Sergeant Sterling McGinnis of Belle Center, Ohio, a hero of three campaigns in the Pacific, sat helpless and heartbroken at her bedside.

News of the atrocious killing spread like wildfire from one end of the island to the other. The populace, military and civilian, was in an uproar, demanding quick and effective police action. A search of the scene where the victim was found led to discovery of her dress and sandals, but no other clues were discovered. It was known that Miss Farnsworth had feared being alone in the jade shop at night and that it was customary for its manager to stay there with her, but on the fatal night he had been called away.

In the absence of clues, the investigation narrowed to a search for suspicious characters. Between fifteen and twenty suspects were rounded up and jailed, but they all denied any knowledge of the crime. The case seemed to be at a standstill, but the plight of the imprisoned suspects remained a serious problem. There was no direct evidence against any of them, and the circumstances that had brought about their detention were weak. While it was obvious that at least some of those in custody were innocent, it was also possible that one of them was a killer. Something had to be done and done quickly. As the authorities faced this dilemma, someone suggested, "Why not use the lie detector? It certainly should provide us with a practical solution."

There was immediate agreement, but it took longer to decide upon the best examiner for the case. Several names were mentioned, but the fame of Lieutenant Riedel of Berkeley had reached across the Pacific, and it was agreed that he was the man for the job.

An immediate appeal for help was made to the Governor of Guam. He, in turn, telephoned Chief of Police John H. Holstrom of Berkeley, asking permission for the immediate transport of Riedel to the troubled island. Permission was quickly granted, but unforeseen difficulties developed and days passed before the trip could be made. Riedel, eager to be of assistance, needed time and further information before embarking. He told those in charge that his lie detector would operate only under 110 alternating current, and he requested that island officials be asked at once if this were available there. Other complications arose as well. Riedel said he must know whether the suspects spoke English and whether they were white or black, explaining that only Caucasians show evidence of blood pressure change when not telling the truth to the polygraph examiner.

The responses were reassuring. The suspects were English-speaking and white. The necessary electric current was available. But then bad weather conditions necessitated a short postpone-ment of the flight. There was still further delay when Riedel's papers from the State Department failed to arrive at the expected time.

When all difficulties had finally been overcome, Riedel hastened aboard the naval flying boat accompanied by his wife. With him he took not one but two lie detectors, for Riedel was a technician who took no chances. One polygraph was borrowed from the Navy; the other was the one he was accustomed to using at Berkeley Police Headquarters.

Arriving on Guam, Riedel reported at once to a former Navy officer named Hackett who was now serving as peace officer on Guam.

Hackett immediately informed his visitor that the number of suspects in custody had been reduced to fifteen.

The body of the murdered Miss Farnsworth had already been put aboard the transport *Thomas Jefferson* to be taken to her parents in San Francisco. Her fiance, Sergeant McGinnis, was given permission to accompany the remains to their destination.

Riedel immediately went into conference with Hackett to review current developments and to plan future strategy. Hackett proposed that Riedel lose no time in testing each of the suspects in custody.

Negative results had been reported from the first few tests when something occurred greatly simplifying Riedel's task. One of the many Guam law enforcement men assigned to the case had by chance discovered Ruth Farnsworth's badly torn smock hidden under the seat of a weapons carrier. It did not take long for the authorities to learn that before the murder the carrier had been driven by Air Force Private Calvin Dennis, aged 25, from Frederick, Maryland.

Young Dennis was sent for and questioned by the authorities. He appeared bewildered by the evidence and said he knew nothing of the murder and could not understand how the garment came to be in the car.

Dennis had not been one of those listed as suspects, and Hackett was amazed when informed of the discovery. "This man, Dennis," he told Riedel, "must be the next to be examined by your lie detector. Of course, I'm suspicious, but the polygraph should be able to tell us whether this is purely a coincidence or whether he is implicated."

Riedel agreed, and hours later the examination of Calvin Dennis was under way. Dennis showed no nervousness, and for a time Riedel thought he had encountered another dead end. But after several hours of questioning, the polygraph began to show surprising results. Obviously, Dennis was not telling the truth. Riedel pressed hard, and soon the graph indicated that he was on the correct trail.

"You are not giving me truthful answers," he told his subject, resorting to the strategy he had used successfully so many times before. "You can't lie to me and get away with it. Now tell me everything you know about this murder—and speak the truth; the instrument will tell me whether you're lying or not."

Dennis' face soon began to betray his emotions. It was apparent that he realized he was trapped and that false answers could be detected. After close to six hours of sparring between Dennis and his examiner, the airman finally blurted: "Guess there's no use lying to you any longer. I was in on it."

"Then let's have the facts—all of them—and truthfully," the polygraphist pressed.

Dennis' next words were a confession. "I was one of them," he admitted, speaking with a show of extreme reluctance.

"And who was with you?" Riedel demanded. "This certainly wasn't a one-man job."

"No, it wasn't," came the response. "There were three of us in on it."

"Speak up. Let's hear who they were."

Dennis hesitated before giving the names of his 20-year-old

half-brother, Herman, and Staff Sergeant Robert W. Burns, a 32-year-old Air Force man from Spokane, Washington.

Then, speaking nonchalantly and with little show of emotion or shame, Calvin Dennis related how he and his two companions, following previously laid plans, had gone to the jade shop under cover of night. They had ripped out the lighting wires, kidnapped the young woman, and carried her kicking and screaming to the secluded area of the darkened jungle. Then he told the revolting details of how she had been beaten, choked, and raped.

Riedel realized that at least half of his mission had been accomplished. He promptly reported to Hackett and his aides who agreed that the next logical step was to test Dennis' half-brother and Burns. The two men, who had previously escaped suspicion, were sent for and told of the contemplated lie detector tests.

Herman Dennis broke down after being told of his half-brother's confession, admitted his guilt, and led officers to the exact location of the crime. Sergeant Burns, however, was harder to handle. Over and over he protested his innocence, despite the fact that the lie detector clearly indicated he was lying. There were obvious discrepancies in his responses, and hours later Riedel reported that Burns had spoken untruthfully in his denials of guilt.

The two Dennis men, in their confession, had implicated another young man, who admitted under the lie detector that he had shared in earlier plans to kidnap and rape Ruth Farnsworth but had suffered from "cold feet" at the eleventh hour and abandoned the others.

Riedel, though gratified by his accomplishment, realized that his work was far from finished. He and Hackett wondered whether any of the other fifteen suspects still in custody might have been implicated. Because of these doubts it was decided that all of them should be examined under the polygraph.

For more than two days a long procession of uniformed men moved slowly into Riedel's temporary polygraph examining quarters. The machine showed their answers to be truthful, and it was agreed that they could be released. The other three, of course, were taken into custody.

What to do next with the Dennis brothers and Burns remained a question. After many conferences, the Air Force agreed to waive jurisdiction, recommending the trio be tried in a civil court subject to Navy observation. They were transferred to a military prison to await trial. Their conviction followed, and the three were sentenced to death. Later it developed that earlier in the investigation, Herman Dennis had been questioned by the military, but "cleared," and allowed to go his way.

For reasons that are neither explained nor recorded, Calvin Dennis' life was spared by President Truman, who commuted the death sentence and decreed that the confessed killer should spend the remainder of his life in prison. He is still confined in a federal prison in the United States.

The day set for execution of the two condemned men, January 28, 1949, finally came. Herman Dennis and Robert Burns followed each other to the gallows and paid with their lives for their fiendish act. The exact time and place of the execution remained a secret.

Before departing for home, Riedel was honored by the Guam authorities at a luncheon hosted by Guam police at their headquarters.

As friendly farewells were spoken, he was warmly praised for his achievement. He and the lie detector were credited with the solution of the ghastly case, and Guam officers admitted that had Riedel not obtained confessions, the investigation well might have ended differently.

18

The Author's Big Scoop

This is a true story of a newspaper scoop, an account of how several enterprising newsmen once scored a "first" by sneaking a lie detector into a jail in the dead of night to test a man accused of murdering a priest. It is related here with due modesty by the man who conceived the idea and carried out the many details essential to a successful execution of the project, and so it will be told in first person.

The mysterious disappearance of Father Patrick Heslin created a sensation in much of California, especially in the San Francisco Bay area. The beloved cleric had been called from his parish house in Colma, a suburb on the southern border of San Francisco, by a strange man who had begged the priest to accompany him to the home of a friend dying of tuberculosis. He wanted the priest to administer the last rites. On that night—August 2, 1921—any drive would have been perilous. Dense fog rolled in from the Pacific, obscuring the torturous corkscrew turns in the roads. Nevertheless, Father Heslin, carrying a bag filled with the items necessary for his mission, tightened his heavy overcoat and set off with the stranger.

On the following morning his housekeeper, Marie Wendell, stared into his room and viewed with alarm the undisturbed bed. Clearly the priest had never returned from his mission. Fearing an accident, she called the town constable, Silvio Landini.

Archbishop Edward J. Hanna of San Francisco was also notified. Posses were hurriedly organized. Believing that the car had swerved off the road and plunged over the precipitous cliffs to the ocean shore below, men combed the area for miles but they found no sign of a wrecked machine.

Word of the mystery spread quickly, and excitement mounted. San Francisco and neighborhood police joined in the hunt, but a day of feverish activity passed with no success. Not a single clue came to light. Not until early that evening were the worst fears justified. It was then that the Archbishop received a special delivery letter, half typewritten and half in penciled script, telling him that the priest was a captive in a "bootleg cellar" and demanding $6,500 in ransom. Instructions for its payment, the writer said, would follow. The letter ended with some ominous words. "Had to hitt [sic] him four times," the postscript read, "and he is unconscious from pressure on the brain, so better hurry and no fooling."

The letter was quickly examined by postal inspectors, who said the postmark showed it to have been mailed in San Francisco only four hours after Father Heslin had been called away. Detectives were posted at the Archbishop's office to intercept any call that might come with further instructions. But no messages came, and police found themselves thwarted because the letter gave no indication as to where the missing priest was being held.

The mystery created a sensation throughout the area. People discussed it everywhere with mounting fears that Father Heslin might not be rescued alive. Huge rewards were offered for information. Long days and nights of search and investigation proved futile. Questionable roominghouses were searched; cars carrying suspicious-looking characters were stopped and their drivers questioned. But after eight days of investigation the police were no nearer a solution than they had been at the outset. And then, by sheer chance and a reporter's resourcefulness, the first break came. George Lynn of the San Francisco *Examiner*, walked into the Archbishop's office in the afternoon looking for news. Sitting nearby was a tall, lanky stranger, middle-aged and bald.

The stranger told an aide that he wished to speak to the

Archbishop and was advised that he would have to wait a short time. "But I'm in a big hurry," the stranger exclaimed angrily. "I can tell him something about Father Heslin—and where to find his body."

The words carried to Lynn's finely tuned ears, and his nose for news was quickly aroused. He moved his chair over to the stranger, identified himself, and asked why the police had not been notified.

"Notify the police!" the man snapped. "I'll have nothing to do with cops." He identified himself as William Hightower, a baker, and agreed to tell the newsman all he knew.

Both men slipped into a private room, where Hightower related the information he said he had received a few nights earlier from a bar girl whom he called Dolly Mason. The girl, he said, had told him about a bootlegger she had met, who had babbled about something he had buried in the sand dunes near Salada Beach close to Colma.

Thinking that the man was referring to bootleg liquor, Dolly Mason had pressed him for details. "Nobody's going to find what I've got down there," the man finally told her. "I've got a partner who fries flapjacks all the time—and he's guarding the spot."

Hightower then stated that he had gone to the beach location several days later. He had once worked near there and remembered seeing a billboard showing a miner frying flapjacks over a campfire.

"And what's all that got to do with Father Heslin?" Lynn interrupted.

"That's what I've been trying to tell you," replied Hightower. "I think the priest is buried there—in the sand below a cliff near that sign. Someone ought to go and look."

"Right," the newsman agreed. "Come with me to my office, and we'll talk it over with my boss, the city editor, Bill Hines." Hightower was willing.

In the *Examiner* office, Hines shook hands with Hightower, then slipped into a private room and summoned Chief of Police Daniel J. O'Brien. O'Brien had listened to only the first part of the story when he concluded that the time for action was at hand. O'Brien, Hightower, Hines, and Lynn immediately started out in a car for the beach. On the way they picked up Constable Landini. Directions came from Hightower, who apparently knew every foot of the way. "Two curves ahead—then stop," he finally ordered as they caught sight of the flapjack billboard.

Leaving the car, he led them over the sand dunes. He approached the edge of a cliff, then jumped to the beach below. The others followed close behind.

"There's the spot," Hightower called out. O'Brien and Landini began shoveling away the loose sand. Suddenly they caught sight of a hand, then a huddled heap in black cloth. It was Father Heslin's body. He appeared to have been struck brutally over the head and shot several times. The coroner was summoned, and after his arrival the party went back to police headquarters.

While *Examiner* presses were grinding out their scoop, O'Brien was grilling Hightower, who insisted he was in no way involved in the murder. Hours of questioning were futile. In the end, Hightower was taken to a cell and charged with murder.

The story provoked wild excitement in the community, with people divided on the issue of Hightower's guilt. Was this all the imagining of a demented man? Was Hightower the actual killer, inventing a fantastic story to cover his guilt? Had he a partner or more accomplices? Could he have killed and buried the priest single-handedly? These were the questions on every tongue. Everyone wondered. So did I.

At the time I was city editor of the San Francisco *Call-Bulletin*, the *Examiner's* sister paper. As I sat at my desk late one night, pondering the questions of the day, the idea came.

I had been reading about experiments in Berkeley with the lie detector. "Why not test Hightower?" I asked myself. But how? He was then being held in the San Mateo County jail in Redwood City, fully forty miles south of San Francisco. The place was swarming with reporters who kept a day and night vigil in case Hightower suddenly confessed or perhaps tried to take his own life. Anything could happen.

I was convinced my idea would work, but first I needed the approval of my superiors. "Go ahead if you can," they said, "but you'll have to carry the ball yourself." Little did I know of the headaches that lay ahead.

First Hightower's lawyer would have to agree; then the consent of San Mateo authorities would be necessary. We would need a lie detector and men to operate it, and, most difficult of all, to score a scoop it would be necessary to thwart the rival newsmen who camped on the courthouse steps until 2 o'clock each morning.

Hightower's attorney gave his consent. "They'll find out he's telling the truth," he told me boastfully. District Attorney, Franklin Swart, had no objections, but he would not interfere with competing newspapermen.

Obtaining a lie detector and an examiner was the next problem. I phoned my good friend, Chief August Vollmer of the Berkeley police, who had been experimenting with the polygraph. He liked the idea. "It would increase interest in the instrument and the technique," he told me. "You'll be hearing from John Larson within the hour."

Larson, who had invented the first polygraph for police use, soon phoned and offered his cooperation. Further arrangements were up to me and for three days and nights I planned the operation. This had to be a scoop, so the test would have to be given after 2 A.M., at which time competing newsmen would be in their beds.

It was finally agreed that Larson, my helpers, and I would assemble in the *Call-Bulletin* office in San Francisco, drive to Redwood City, and wait there at the home of our circulation manager, John Grey, until the vital hour.

Our dramatic night finally came. John Larson arrived with his equipment and one of his assistants. Philips Edson. We had previously decided that the man to witness the test and report it for our paper would be Elford Eddy, a veteran reporter with a gift for diction and keen observation.

After a quick dinner that seemed endless, we piled into the car and started for Redwood City. We discussed little else but our contemplated scoop as the evening hours wore on. At last the hands of the clock showed 2 A.M. It was time to go.

Fortunately, our party found the courthouse stairs clear of newsmen. We had feared that if any overstayed his assigned hours, the test would have to be postponed. By prearranged plan, we were welcomed by the jailers and led to Hightower's cell. He was awakened and informed that the test had the approval of his lawyer. This word removed any doubt from his mind; the examination might even prove his truthfulness, he obviously thought.

Larson and Edson began their preparations. Larson would pose the questions, and he had prepared them meticulously. With no mention of the Heslin case, he began by asking: "Do you smoke, Mr. Hightower?" and "Are you fond of reading?" As the prisoner answered, the recording pens maintained a steady line on the graph.

More inquiries of the same unrelated nature followed with unchanged results. Then came Larson's "dynamite" question. "Did you kill Father Heslin?" he demanded without warning.

"No," came the quick and emphatic answer. Suddenly the recording pens slipped from their steady course and shot upward, nearly jumping over the edge of the recording paper. It was the answer for which the expert had been waiting.

More direct and pertinent questions followed with the same result. An hour later the test was over and Larson reported to us that beyond doubt Hightower had lied in trying to vindicate himself. Now we had a scoop.

The next afternoon the story covered the front page under the banner EXTRA. It was a difficult story to put on paper, but Eddy had done his best with the following account:

> Science penetrated the inscrutable face of William Hightower today, revealing that beneath an unruffled exterior is a seething torment of heart-throbbing emotions and that these emotions indicate strongly that he was the murderer of Father Heslin of Colma.
>
> During the small hours of the morning a scientific 'soul test' was administered to Hightower in the San Mateo County jail.
>
> This was the most remarkable bit of psychological research undertaken on this coast, in which an apparatus known as a sphygmomanometer was relied upon to determine the truth or falsity of the statements of a man charged with murder, a man whose life is at stake.
>
> The apparatus, which records heart throbs and blood pressure, was called on to perform a new miracle of chemistry—the chemistry of psychology—in which a soul was laid bare and subjected to the critical inspection of seekers after truth.
>
> And before the test was concluded this apparatus was to

tear the mask of self-control from the unfathomable face of William Hightower and to show him to the investigators as the man he is—not the cool, calculating dauntless man he has been regarded, but a man torn with human passions, fears, human frailties—cringing inwardly while wearing a mask of iron. . . . Dr. Larson's experiment has been tried and proved 100 percent efficient.

The story created a sensation, and no longer did the public doubt the man's guilt. While the police reserved official comment on the lie detector and its results, they moved with lightning speed to clinch their case. Apparently Larson's conclusions had left them more certain than ever that they were dealing with a guilty man.

Searching Hightower's room in a cheap lodging house, the police found a strange array of firearms and ammunition. Hidden under the bed lay a crude weapon consisting of ten short lengths of pipe, each loaded with a shotgun shell. Nearby lay a machine gun and a gas mask. In another part of the room was a folded tent. Scrawled over one of its folds was the word *tuberculosis*. Detectives surmised that the kidnapped priest had been kept captive under the tent before being murdered. Elsewhere were sheets of paper on which Hightower had scrawled romantic poetry.

For a scientific evaluation of their evidence, the police enlisted the services of a Berkeley criminologist, Edward O. Heinrich, who did much to strengthen the case against Hightower. He analyzed grains of sand adhering to the folded tent and concluded that they were precisely the same as the sand in which the body lay. His microscopic examination of a pocketknife found in Hightower's trousers revealed tiny cotton fibers which matched white string tied to lengths of lumber in the grave. The police were convinced that they now had more incriminating evidence than they needed.

Weeks later Hightower faced a jury in Redwood City Superior Court. The lie detector conclusions were not offered in evidence, for they would have been inadmissible, but in a short time the accused man was found guilty. He was sentenced to life inprisonment in San Quentin Penitentiary, where he spent most of his remaining lifetime before being paroled a few years ago.

The Truth Will Out

A lie detector in the hands of a competent examiner once helped free a falsely convicted man who had already served sixteen years in a Michigan penitentiary. The final vindication was also a victory for a widely publized group of dedicated men who spent their own time and money investigating puzzling cases in an effort to make sure that justice was done. Their founder was the late Erle Stanley Gardner, celebrated author of crime mysteries and creator of the legendary Perry Mason. If not for the determination of this group, Louis Gross would probably have remained in prison for the remainder of his life.

Gross' long story of suffering and frustration began one night in November 1932, when Martado Abrahams, a middle-aged Syrian peddler, was found murdered in his bedroom in Highland Park, a Detroit suburb. Abrahams had been shot through the forehead with a revolver.

The motive for the crime remained a mystery, although detectives suspected the killing might have been related to a romance between Abrahams' estranged wife, Xamid, and a man who, since he was never prosecuted, will be referred to only as Mr. Jones. Detectives reasoned that Abrahams might have interfered in the love affair. The couple was questioned, but both denied any knowledge of the murder.

The first tangible clue in the case came from Jones. Under severe grilling, he told the police that during his initial questioning he had forgotten to reveal an essential detail of importance.

"This peddler, Louis Gross, told me that he shot Abrahams," Jones declared.

"Did Gross tell you why he did it?" the officers inquired.

"It was something about a rug Gross had sold to Abrahams and which was not paid for," Jones explained. "I was told, that Gross, failing to collect from Mrs. Abrahams, said, 'I'll kill your old man if he doesn't pay me.' "

Gross was later interrogated for many hours, but he stoutly denied ever making such a statement. He insisted he knew nothing about the murder. In fact, he turned the tables on Jones, declaring that the latter had offered him jewelry worth $150 if he would "take care" of Abrahams.

Continuing their investigation of the murder, police soon learned that Gross had recently been involved in an alleged theft. Although detectives had no other evidence against him in the Abrahams affair, he was arrested and charged with the killing.

Ten months elapsed before Gross was brought to trial before Judge DeWitt M. Miriam in Detroit. Jones, a star witness for the state, repeated his previous accusations against Gross. Additional witnesses presented other damaging testimony.

In rebuttal, Gross' lawyer introduced an alibi, supported by several witnesses who swore that the accused man had been playing cards with them at the apparent time of the murder. This favorable testimony was later shattered by rebuttal witnesses, and Gross was finally found guilty of murder and sentenced to life imprisonment.

Gross continued to plead his innocence, but with few friends and little money there was not much he could do. Two years later, a deputy in the office of the new district attorney received an appealing letter from Gross. His curiosity aroused, the deputy decided to look into the matter. He turned to the files for the records of the case but could not find them. His interest probably would have impelled him to look further had not other and more pressing matters demanded his attention.

The years passed, and Gross became a victim of tuberculosis

and was moved to the prison hospital. What he then considered a misfortune eventually proved to be one of the luckiest turns in his life, for in the prison hospital he met Rabbi Joshua S. Sperka. The rabbi often visited prisoners in the hospital, hoping to cheer them and to care for a few of their personal wants. Listening to Gross' grim story, the rabbi was deeply impressed and promised to do whatever he could to help.

Rabbi Sperka, knowing of the dedicated and effective work of what was then known as the Court of Last Resort, lost no time in contacting its head, Erle Stanley Gardner. He requested that the group look into the case. By then, Gross had been in prison for sixteen years.

Gardner believed that Gross' situation warranted inquiry and discussed the case with Dr. LeMoyne Snyder, a forensic medical man and a colleague in the Court of Last Resort. They decided to fly to Detroit and meet Rabbi Sperka, whose obvious concern for Gross moved them to visit the prisoner himself. They talked for hours with Gross, who dwelt at length on his innocence and on his inability to prove it. His story was convincing, although the visitors were inclined to be a bit skeptical because they knew of Gross' previous difficulties with the law.

Nevertheless, the two men left the prison convinced that the case called for further investigation and that the basic facts together with their progress should be reported monthly in Henry Steeger's magazine, *The Argosy,* so the public might follow developments. They also arranged to meet with Gerald K. O'Brien, who was then the prosecutor of Wayne County and was somewhat familiar with the case. To their surprise, Gardner and Dr. Snyder found O'Brien eager to launch an official inquiry into the matter. He explained that as a prosecutor it was his duty to look into any possible miscarriage of justice.

Almost immediately, O'Brien and the men from the Court made a shocking discovery. All of Gross' trial records were missing, and it was apparent they had been deliberately removed by someone eager to thwart any reopening of the case. Only a single document recording Gross' conviction and sentence remained in the files. Even the court reporter's notes had been torn from his books.

Mystified by this turn of events, O'Brien promptly assigned

three of his best men to participate in an investigation. As the inquiry progressed, the investigators met a retired police captain, William I. Cross. They had been told that Cross, long before, had interested himself in the question of Gross' guilt but had been thwarted in his inquiries by a powerful politician who had warned him to "lay off." Captain Cross readily became a new ally, explaining that he was convinced of Gross' innocence and would be glad to assist in any investigation. His disclosures quickly added new mystery to the case.

Cross told the investigators that the warning from the politician had come while he was checking into the background of a new murder suspect in the Abrahams killing. After ignoring this warning, he had been summoned to headquarters and told bluntly that it was time for him to retire, that his services were no longer needed. He had no alternative but to comply.

The captain, however, now insisted on joining the Court of Last Resort investigators, and together they uncovered enough new evidence to justify a possible theory as to the true motive of the Abrahams murder. They learned that unlimited gambling had been going on in certain protected areas of Detroit, that Abrahams had been losing money at the card tables, and that he'd probably been killed because of his failure to pay his debts. This, they reasoned, might explain the desire of his assassins to hinder an inquiry by removing the official records.

Into such a grimly complicated background, Gross' principal accuser, Mr. Jones, fitted well. He was widely known as an underworld figure who associated with gamblers and racketeers. The investigators surmised that he was probably involved in a plot to frame Gross and keep him behind bars.

O'Brien now proposed a bold move. "If Jones perjured himself in accusing Gross, we should know about it," he told the others. "His truthfulness in his sworn testimony is something that we should look into."

"Just how would you go about that?" Gardner inquired.

"It's very simple," O'Brien told him. "We must insist on having Jones examined under a lie detector. That should determine his truthfulness on the stand when he appeared as the chief witness against Gross. He certainly can't lie to the polygraph without branding himself a perjurer."

"Is that test you talk about something that can be done?" Gardner asked.

"Why not?" the prosecutor retorted.

Jones was summoned to the district attorney's office and told of O'Brien's request. His response was a blunt refusal. "I've told under oath exactly what I know," he protested. "Why must my truthfulness be questioned? Are you implying that I'm a liar?"

"That's exactly what we want to find out," O'Brien said, reminding Jones that if he had spoken the truth in court, he had nothing to lose by repeating his testimony.

At length, Jones reluctantly agreed to undergo the test. He was taken to the office of an expert polygraphist and prepared for the examination. Jones looked on sullenly as the straps were adjusted around his body and the armcuff put in place. "You're treating me like a criminal," he protested.

The examiner began in the usual manner to establish a level for the graph, asking a number of innocuous questions—the size of Jones' shoes, his smoking preferences, and his normal bedtime. Jones grew more angry and sullen with each question.

Then came the all-important inquiry: "Did Louis Gross ever tell you that he had murdered Martado Abrahams?"

The reply came without a second's hesitation. "Yes, he certainly did. That's precisely what I said in court."

At that moment the recording pens jerked violently; then they jumped upward sharply, rising almost to the outer edge of the graph pages. There could be only one conclusion—the answer was a lie!

Realizing the importance of what he had just seen, the polygraphist eagerly sought to verify his conclusion. Resuming with a volley of unrelated questions, he came again to the all-important one. The result was the same. Now he was fully satisfied there had been no error.

Gardner and his colleagues were excited by reports of the test, but they wondered whether immediate action would be wise. They were still trying to identify the politician who had warned Captain Cross to cease his activities on Gross' behalf and who was probably responsible for the missing records. They finally decided that their most important responsibility was to bring the results of the lie detector test to the attention of the proper authorities. After all, Gross' vindication was their major goal. Gardner and O'Brien appeared before Judge Thomas J. Maher of the Wayne County Circuit Court to report their findings and to request a reconsideration of the motion to grant Gross a retrial, a motion that had been made and denied many years earlier. To Gardner and O'Brien's delight, Judge Maher agreed to hold a formal hearing on the motion on October 28, 1949, only a few days hence.

On that morning Louis Gross was led, heavily manacled, into a crowded courtroom. Word of the intended proceedings had become known, and an account of the lie detector test had appeared in the morning newspapers. When the case was called, O'Brien was the first to speak. Talking slowly and with marked emphasis, he told the judge that he intended to argue first for a new trial. If this were granted, he would then move for a dismissal of the charges against Gross, for he had no intention of subjecting the man to a second trial.

Referring frequently to a sheaf of papers in his hand, the prosecutor reviewed the investigation from its beginning, climaxing his argument with the charge that Mr. Jones had deliberately given false testimony. To prove this, he offered to put the polygraph examiner on the stand, a request which was finally refused.

Judge Maher interrupted occasionally to ask for further information, referring to Captain Cross' forced retirement and the order he had received to "lay off" the Gross case. The surprise of the day came when Judge Maher announced that he intended to rule at once, for it had been expected he would take the matter under advisement. He prefaced his decision by reviewing each point O'Brien had made and concluded with a comment that amazed his listeners.

"It appears to me that Louis Gross has been framed!" he said, before announcing that he would grant Gross a retrial. Then he complimented those who had carried on the long investigation, paying especial tribute to O'Brien's "diligent work" and calling the prosecutor an official "who believes his job is not only to prosecute the guilty but to protect the innocent."

It was now O'Brien's move. He promptly called for a dismissal of the murder charge against Gross, and the court immediately assented. After sixteen years in the penitentiary, Gross, quickly unshackled, turned to shake hands with those who had made his vindication possible.

As for Mr. Jones, he escaped prosecution as a perjurer because the polygraph test that branded him a liar would not be admissible in court. Some even suspected that he was the murderer of Abrahams, but in the judgment of the investigators the evidence was not sufficient to warrant prosecution.

Gardner, O'Brien, and their colleagues in the investigation were content that they had righted a miscarriage of justice. The lie detector had proved its worth, and Gross' main accuser was branded as a perjurer even though he escaped prosecution.

The actual killer of Abrahams was never apprehended.

On the other side of the continent, in California, 33-year-old Willie M. Anderson of Marin City, on the north side of San Francisco Bay, narrowly escaped a fate similar to that of Louis Gross. Trapped in a tight web of incriminating circumstances, Anderson was arrested on the complaint of a 13-year-old girl who told Deputy Sheriff Fred Hooper that she had been threatened with death and robbed of $60 by a strange man while enroute to the post-office to buy a money order for her mother.

After relating her experiences to Hooper, the girl was asked if she could describe the robber in detail. "Of course I can," she answered readily. "I purposely took a very good look at him." She pictured the holdup man, giving his approximate age, height, and weight, and a description of his clothing.

The officer pressed for still more imformation. "Didn't you notice any extraordinary details?" he inquired. "Anything like a scar or a mole that would help us to identify him?"

"I can tell you what his car looked like," she volunteered.

"But nothing more?" Hooper asked.

The little girl's face brightened. "Oh yes," she added. "Would this help? I noticed a torn sleeve in his leather jacket. I'd recognize that tear anywhere. It wasn't exactly the kind of a tear you'd expect to see in that kind of a coat."

Hooper, a man for details, took a piece of paper from his pocket and jotted down a few notes. The description, including the detail of the torn sleeve, was passed to other deputy sheriffs in and around Marin City, and a thorough search began.

On the following morning Hooper's attention was drawn to a

man standing beside a downtown show window. Looking closer, he noticed a close resemblance to the wanted man. Parked at the curb close by was a car like the one the girl had described.

"Come with me," Hooper directed as he approached the stranger. "I have a few questions I'd like to ask you at the station."

"Like what?"

"You look a lot like a man we want for the robbery of a little girl. I'd like to take a look in your home."

"That's all right with me, mister," the man replied, "but you'll find out you've got the wrong man. I don't go around robbing little girls." He said his name was Willie Anderson.

Together they walked to Anderson's home. Hooper talked to Anderson's wife, and began a search of the place. In the bedroom hung a leather jacket like the one that had been described. The deputy examined it closely, noting that one of the sleeves was torn in exactly the way the child had mentioned.

"That's just a coincidence," Anderson protested.

"Well, then, can you tell me exactly where you were yesterday afternoon?"

The man shrugged his shoulders.

Half an hour later Anderson was in a cell in the San Rafael jail, charged with robbery. Hooper was certain he had an open-and-shut case.

A day later Anderson appeared in court for arraignment, still claiming that he was the victim of a serious mistake. He approached District Attorney W. O. Weissich, pleaded his innocence, and asked if he might undergo a lie detector test to prove it.

"You have that right," the prosecutor told him. "Tomorrow we'll go to San Francisco and see a polygraphist that I trust. "If you're really innocent, I want to know it."

Handcuffed, Anderson was taken across the bay to the Market Street offices of George W. Harman, who for many years had operated as a private polygraphist. Weissich told him the details of the case. Meanwhile, back in Marin City, Deputy Hooper was again questioning the little girl in an attempt to verify her original complaint. Her story was precisely the same.

Hours later, in Harman's office, Hooper was amazed to hear

the results of the lie detector examination. "I can't detect a single flaw in the test," Harman told him. "We've gone over all of the questions, one after the other, and the graph shows positively that every answer is correct. I really think he must be innocent."

Suddenly doubting his "open-and-shut case," Hooper returned to Marin City to question the child again. As he told her of the polygraph test, he noticed tears in the little girl's eyes.

"If you're not telling me the truth, you'd better admit it," he told her sharply. "Tell the truth, and I promise you won't be punished."

"You mean that?"

"Of course I do."

Then the supposed robbery victim broke down and admitted she had not told the truth. "I lost the money on the way to the post office," she sobbed, wiping her cheeks with a handkerchief. "I didn't want to be punished at home, so I just made up that robbery story. Now you know what really happened—it's the whole truth."

"Where'd you get that description of the robber from?" Hooper demanded. "All that stuff about the torn sleeve."

She said she had seen Anderson on the street that morning, that she had never seen him before but had simply described him to make her robbery complaint look good.

Anderson was escorted to court with his accuser. Addressing Municipal Judge N. Charles Brusatori, the girl related her story, and Assistant District Attorney Roger Garety moved that the charges against Anderson be dismissed. The judge turned the girl over to juvenile authorities and granted the motion for Anderson's vindication.

"Beyond doubt," Garety told the court, "Anderson would have been convicted on the evidence and sent to prison."

Judge Brusatori smiled as he looked down at Deputy Hooper and polygraphist Harman. "Let me officially congratulate you both," he said. "You did a perfect job in the interest of justice, and you have the thanks of this court."

A Case of Overconfidence

A defendant who demands a lie detector test to prove his innocence may later regret it, for the test may wind up proving his guilt instead. Such was the case of Charles Oliver Coston, a robbery suspect in Baltimore in the fall of 1971. He took a polygraph examination at his own request—and, as a result, found himself sentenced to a long prison term.

The crime of which Coston insisted he was innocent took place about 9:25 P.M. on August 8, 1970. The victim was Hope Okeke, a native Manchurian and a student at Morgan State College. Okeke drove a cab in his spare time to finance his schooling. At the time of the crime young Okeke was looking for a fare in the area of Woodbourne Avenue and York Road when he slowed down for a red light at an intersection. Peering through his cab window, he caught sight of a tall pedestrian signaling for him to stop. As he did so, a young man hurried toward the cab, opened the door, and took a front seat beside the driver.

"Where to?" asked Okeke. His passenger gave him one address, suggesting that instead of following the usual route, he take a shortcut through a different area where the traffic would be lighter.

Passenger and cabbie were well on their way when Okeke felt a cold, hard object against his right ear. Glancing furtively in that direction, he was horrified to see a revolver held against his head.

"Hand over your cash and do it fast," the gunman commanded, emphasizing his order with a string of profane oaths.

Realizing the futility of resistance, Okeke reached into his coat pocket, took out all the money he'd earned that night ($42), and handed it to his passenger without comment.

"Get yourself out of here now," the bandit directed. "Just run down the road with your back to the cab. I'll take over at the wheel, and you'll find this old bus at some place where I decide to dump it."

Okeke did as he was told. Glancing back as he ran, he saw the taxi speed off in the other direction. A while later, in a different section of the city, Okeke saw a police officer on a corner and reported the crime. He gave the policeman a detailed description of the robber, explaining that he'd gotten a good look at the man who had been standing near a street light when he stopped the cab.

The description of the gunman was flashed by teletype to all district police stations, and patrolmen were ordered to search for such a person and to arrest him if he could not give a satisfactory account of himself. A number of suspects were picked up, questioned, and released after explaining their movements.

Okeke, lamenting the loss of his money, feared that the bandit would never be captured. He conferred from time to time with the police and was told that everything possible was being done. The young student, however, resolved to keep his own lookout for the holdup man. There were many times in various places where he thought a stranger resembled the fugitive, but in every case he found some discrepancy in the exact description he had memorized. In fact, on two or three occasions he actually approached a suspect with a question or two, only to discover on closer observation that it wasn't the right man.

Nearly a month had passed without success when the unexpected occurred. On the night of September 1, Okeke was obliged to appear in Baltimore's traffic court to testify as a witness to an accident. As he looked about, seeking the officer to whom he had been told to report, his attention was attracted by a group of about fifteen men crowded together and talking in a nearby hallway. Glancing curiously in that direction, Okeke's eyes fell on one of the bystanders and cold shivers suddenly ran up his spine. "That's him," he told himself. "I could recognize him in any crowd."

Cautiously, and careful to conceal his excitement, Okeke edged his way toward the little group for a closer look at the man he suspected. With extreme care lest he be observed, he viewed the stranger's profile and physique. "It's him all right," he thought, determined not to allow such an opportunity to slip through his fingers.

Looking quickly about for a policeman, his eyes fell on Officer Thomas Floyd, and he hurriedly approached the bluecoat. "There's a man over there in that little crowd in the hallway who robbed me a few weeks ago in my cab," he said. "Arrest him. I'll gladly swear to the charge."

"Are you really sure of yourself?" Floyd inquired. "Robbery, you know, is a serious charge."

"I know that, Officer," Okeke replied. "I had an unusually good look at this man when he robbed me. The light was bright. Really, I'd recognize him anywhere. I've been scouting around for him for weeks."

Admittedly perplexed and unwilling to become involved in a false arrest, Officer Floyd directed Okeke to step cautiously toward his suspect and look again more carefully.

Okeke was back minutes later. "I'm positive it's him," he reported. "I understand how serious this matter is."

The policeman moved toward the group and dropped his hand lightly on the stranger's shoulder. "Better come with me," he said. "You're under arrest."

"What for?" the other snapped. "I didn't do anything wrong; you're picking on the wrong man." He said that his name was Charles Coston and that he had never been in trouble.

Floyd telephoned for a patrol wagon and escorted Coston to the Baltimore City jail. Young Okeke accompanied them. At the jail the booking sergeant asked Okeke if he was certain of his identification. The cabman assured him that there was no mistake, and Coston was booked on a charge of robbery.

On the following day he appeared before Judge Paul A. Dorf in Criminal Court of Baltimore and pleaded not guilty. Speaking to his attorney, he was bitter and pugnacious in asserting his innocence. "Don't you know it's my word against that cab driver," he argued. "Will the judge believe his word against mine?"

"That's for the judge to decide," the attorney said.

Coston scratched his head for a moment, and his eyes brightened. "Say, I've got a great idea," he blurted. "A few years ago a guy I knew was busted for something he said he hadn't done, and you know how he beat it?"

"How?"

"He simply took one of those lie detector tests and told the fellow who gave it that he was innocent. The examiner told the judge that the guy was telling the truth when he said he wasn't guilty, and the judge turned him loose right then and there. Why couldn't I do the same thing?"

"You mean you want to take a lie detector test?" the attorney asked.

"You said it," Coston asserted. "I'll say I didn't rob that cab driver. The machine will show that I'm telling the truth, and I'll be out of this mess."

"My boy, you'll be taking a mighty big chance," replied the lawyer. "You can't beat those lie detectors, you know. If it should happen that you're really guilty and you say you're not, the machine will show that you're lying and you'll be cooked like a roasted duck. Do you really want to take a chance like that?"

"Who says I'm taking a chance?" the other snapped. "No chance at all. I can prove by this lie detector that I'm telling the truth, and I'll be out of here faster than even you can spring me."

"If you want to take a gamble like that, it's your liberty you're playing with," the lawyer cautioned. "We'll speak to the judge. It's up to him, you know."

The request for a lie detector test was presented to Judge Dorf, who listened carefully and then addressed the defendant. He explained that the court had no legal power to compel a defendant to take a polygraph test. However, he stated, if the district attorney were willing and if the defendant agreed to allow the test results, favorable or unfavorable, to be introduced in evidence at the trial, permission would be granted. Coston grinned and nodded his assent.

Counsel for both sides then conferred, eager to agree on a suitable and experienced polygraph examiner. Half an hour later they had picked the man they wanted, an operator of recognized ability and experience.

Coston, still maintaining an air of complete confidence, met the polygraphist a day later in a quiet room at City Hall. The test proceeded along customary lines, with the accused man vigorously denying he had robbed the cab driver. The same question of guilt was asked over and over. Each time the answer was the same. Before long the examination was over.

As the straps were being removed from Coston's body, he looked up at the examiner with a satisfied grin. "Guess I passed this pretty good, didn't I?" he said.

The polygraphist dodged the question. "It's my duty to report the results to the judge," he replied nonchalantly, reassembling his apparatus.

Had Coston known the results, he would not have been so pleased with himself. Judge Dorf was told that in the operator's best judgment Coston "had attempted to deceive in his replies to certain questions pertaining directly to the robbery."

After taking careful note of this report and making a number of inquiries regarding the technique used, Judge Dorf commented that he faced no alternative but to proceed with the trial, which he would conduct without a jury. He said that aside from the negative nature of the report, he was not wholly satisfied with the manner in which the test was conducted. He did not indicate what course he would have taken had the test report been favorable.

After Okeke had testified for the state, again identifying the accused as the robber, Coston took the stand in his own defense, swearing that on the evening of the holdup, he was at the home of a friend, Herbert Johns, playing pool with his host and two girls. He had arrived at the house at 7 P.M., he swore, and remained there until 10:30. His alibi completely covered the time of the holdup. However, to Coston's chagrin, he could produce no witnesses to corroborate his alibi.

"Why would I have turned robber for forty-two dollars?" he asked from the witness chair. "I was working for a construction company that paid me from a hundred and ten to a hundred fifteen dollars a week. I had been laid off, but during the week of August 8 they were paying me fifty-five dollars."

With a stern frown on his face, Judge Dorf looked down from the bench. He stated that although he would not be influenced by the unfavorable polygraph test, he found himself obliged to give credence to Okeke's testimony which positively identified the accused as the gunman. His conclusions, he said, were not altered by the fact that Okeke, in reporting the robbery to the police, had pictured the holdup man as being six feet tall, whereas Coston actually measured six-foot-seven. Allowances should be made for such a discrepancy, the judge ruled, commenting that the victim had a poor chance to estimate his passenger's exact height.

In conclusion, the judge found Coston guilty as charged and sentenced him to ten years in prison. There was an immediate appeal, but the higher court upheld Judge Dorf's decision in every respect.

The Tillinger Affair

I n 1920 the Tillinger case became an international sensation on two continents as thousands of people, Jews and non-Jews alike, tried to locate a man who had disappeared after spreading false and highly defamatory charges against the Jewish people. Tillinger's accusations were believed by anti-Semites in Europe, and his canard spread with the rapidity of a forest fire. His accusations were accepted as truth in many quarters, provoking violence. There were pogroms in many areas and massacres that produced a death toll reaching into the hundreds.

Jewish resentment rose rapidly, and leaders of large European Jewish communities resolved to meet their accuser and impress upon him his responsibility for the tragedies that were occurring. But Tillinger could not be found.

Jewish organizations with many resources and much volunteer help took charge of the search. The object of the hunt, which extended throughout Europe and across the Atlantic to the United States, was an aging man thought to be Tillinger in disguise. Time and again it was belived that Tillinger had been caught in the net, but somehow the wanted man always seemed to slip through the mesh. Months passed with reports of the fugitive coming in from one American city after another. Tillinger was said to be traveling under different aliases and under heavy disguise.

At one point the trail led to Youngstown, Ohio, but again the searchers were thwarted. Frequently Tillinger was reported to be in eastern cities, working as a janitor in various synagogues; but the trails and the clues invariably proved useless.

Jewish leaders were about ready to abandon their fruitless hunt when an unexpected message came from the West Coast. In Oakland, California, a stranger had appeared at one of the city's largest synagogues and asked for any kind of manual work that would provide food and shelter. A kindly looking person in his late years, he humbly explained that he had little education and was not qualified for more than cleaning work. He got the job.

Members of the congregation slowly came to know and like him and to sympathize with his apparent loneliness. But those who talked with him soon found themselves disturbed by obvious and significant contradictions in his story. Although he repeatedly lamented his lack of schooling, his conversation betrayed considerable education and he showed a surprising familiarity with publications widely read by European rabbis.

Suspicion was aroused, and people began to wonder if this stranger could possibly be Tillinger. They questioned him, cautiously at first, but he was firm in his insistence that he was not the wanted man. In fact, he claimed to know nothing of the mysterious and elusive bigot. Then one daring person snapped a picture of the man and sent it to New York leaders familiar with the case. Their response was that without doubt this stranger was Tillinger. Confronted with this report, the janitor became angry, insisting more vehemently than before that he was not the fugitive. To support his denials, he gave the synagogue leaders the names and addresses of several people in New York City. He said these were relatives with whom he had stayed and vowed that they would quickly support his position. But all efforts to locate the supposed kin came to naught, and some of those contacted said they had never heard of the man.

The search had come to a halt when a strange coincidence occurred. A rabbi in nearby Berkeley was being coerced by his 10-year-old son for a chance to visit the Berkeley Police Department. The rabbi, unable to resist his boy's pleas, finally contacted Chief August Vollmer, head of the Berkeley force, and an invitation followed.

Instructed by Vollmer to make the visit as enjoyable and educational as possible, officers outdid themselves. In the course of the tour, they showed the boy the lie detector machine that had been developed in response to the chief's suggestions and explained its workings. The lad was fascinated.

That night at dinner the youngster described what he had seen. "Say, Dad," he suggested, "why don't you ask them to examine that man who works at the synagogue in Oakland? I'll bet he'll turn out to be Tillinger."

The father, deeply impressed, thought it was a fine idea. With the concurrence of other synagogue leaders, he communicated with Vollmer, who listened eagerly to a recital of the circumstances and said he would be glad to have one of his experts conduct the examination.

Vollmer called in the man who had developed the first polygraph and knew all of the techniques involved in its use, Dr. John Larson, Vollmer's working partner in the new project.

The mysterious janitor was told of the plan. Although some believed he would object, he surprised them by saying he would be glad to prove his innocence through a scientific procedure. In fact, he wondered whether a number of those who suspected him of untruthfulness might not be invited to witness the test. This was quickly arranged, and only days later a group of synagogue members sat together in the polygraph room at police headquarters. Eagerly awaiting the start of the test, a few openly predicted that the lie detector would unmask the subject and expose him as Tillinger. Excitement mounted as one man exclaimed in a voice audible throughout the tense room: "We are all 99 percent convinced that he's Tillinger, but we need confirmation before going any further. And we're going to get confirmation today—that's a certainty." Others echoed his words and agreed strongly with his urge for fair play. "He deserves a fair chance," they all said.

Before undertaking the examination, Larson warned those present to remain quiet. His request, however, went unheeded by the subject. Turning to those who had come to see and listen, he shouted, "You say I'm Tillinger, but I'm not. You lie. You want my honesty tested; that's why I'm here. You'll see."

Larson hastened to complete the necessary preliminaries and began his questioning, which lasted for nearly three hours, and went something like this:

"Have you ever been in Europe?"

"Yes."

"And have you lived in New York City?"

"Yes, I have."

"Are you Tillinger?"

"No!" the answer was emphatic.

When the janitor was asked a second time, somewhat later, if he was Tillinger, the reply was the same. Larson, closely watching the graphs on the recording paper of the polygraph, noted that they did not change at all when his subject answered the vital question.

At last Larson unstrapped the man and turned to his small and unusual audience. "Gentlemen," he announced, "this man has spoken the truth. He is not Tillinger. Of that I am certain now."

Those who had watched the test looked amazed. They told the man who had been their suspect to return to his job, that they were satisfied with what the test had disclosed.

Vollmer and Larson received the written thanks of the congregation and its leaders. The police chief replied graciously, saying he was gratified that the machine in which he was so interested had actually proved its worth in helping an innocent person.

The old man returned to his menial work in the synagogue, and friendships that had waned were soon renewed, perhaps with greater warmth. But the janitor knew nothing of the happy sequel that was soon to follow. One morning, nearly a month later, he appeared at work with a young man at his side, introducing him as his son. The son explained that in Los Angeles he had heard of his father's difficulties and had hastened north to offer explanations. "I just wanted you all to know who Dad really is," said the son. "He's been a wanderer all his life and has become separated from me and the rest of the family."

A few of his listeners quickly arranged an impromptu luncheon, and the father and son became honored guests. The old man beamed graciously and thanked his hosts.

Defeat for a "Good Samaritan"

Wallace A. H. Wochnick of Los Angeles considered himself a good samaritan. The district attorney called him a murderer. A lie detector examiner, to whom Wochnick looked confidently for vindication, called him a liar.

The final determination, which came only after an appeal and two jury trials, hardly pleased Wochnick, who had not expected the trial judge to permit the introduction of unfavorable polygraph testimony.

The murder victim was James Kibrick, proprietor of a liquor store on the corner of Temple and Freemont Streets in Los Angeles. The crime occurred on a winter morning in 1950 and was witnessed by no one but the killer. The state's star witness was Philip Anast, one of Kibrick's customers, who had summoned the police to the scene and provided detectives with the only details on which the charge against Wochnick was based. There was a wide discrepancy between the testimony of the two men.

Anast told the police that he had called at the liquor store to make a delivery and found Kibrick lying on his back behind the counter in what appeared to be a pool of blood. He also claimed to have seen a man, later identified as Wochnick, straddling the victim's legs in a squatting position. At first, he said, it appeared to him as if Wochnick was unbuttoning the shirt front of the victim.

"He's been badly beaten," Wochnick had told Anast, pointing to the shattered liquor bottles which would account for the bleeding wounds about the fallen man's head, face, and hands. Only later did the coroner decide that the actual cause of death was a wound from a knife that had been plunged into Kibrick's chest, piercing his heart. The knife, it was later learned, belonged to the storekeeper and had customarily been kept beside the cash register, obviously for protection.

Anast told the officers that on seeing the dying man on the floor and hearing from Wochnick that a brutal crime had been committed, he had run out of the place to summon help. On his return he saw the victim seated in a chair between the counter and a stack of shelves loaded with liquor bottles. As he looked more closely at the dying man, he observed what he first took to be a cigar butt protruding from the storekeeper's shirt. But on second sight it proved to be the taped handle of a knife. Kibrick died on the way to the hospital, and Wochnick took credit for what he said had been humanitarian service to a badly wounded stranger.

Wochnick's story to detectives was widely different from Anast's. Confronted with Anast's account, he reasoned that the discrepancies were likely due to nervousness and shock. Wochnick informed the police that on entering the liquor store to make a delivery for his employers, he had seen no one and that as he turned his back toward the street a strange man had brushed past him running toward the open front door. Then he said he had heard a sharp moan from behind the counter. Looking in that direction, he had observed Kibrick lying on the floor. He had assumed that the departing man was the murderer. Eager to assist the wounded man. Wochnick said he had dropped to one knee and begun brushing splintered glass away from the shopkeeper, whom he tried unsuccessfully to lift to a sitting position. It was during this futile effort that Anast first appeared.

The police seriously doubted Wochnick's account, and after considerable questioning of Anast and Wochnick, the latter was arrested and charged with murder.

Wochnick protested his innocence and volunteered to take a lie detector test to prove it. A police officer named Zander was assigned to give Wochnick the test. Zander's final report of the examination, which he made to Judge J. Wilson, disclosed his conclusion that Wochnick had not been altogether truthful in his replies to questions. There were discrepancies, he said, which led to his belief that his subject had failed the test. But it was not so much the test as the conversation between Zander and Wochnick after the examination that ultimately led to a legal controversy.

On the basis of Zander's report, the judge directed that Wochnick stand trial before a jury for murder. He allowed Officer Zander to appear as a witness so that he could tell judge and jury why he did not believe the defendant had been truthful. This testimony deeply impressed the jury, which found Wochnick guilty of first degree murder. He was then sentenced to life in prison.

Defense counsel immediately moved for a retrial, contending that the trial judge had erred in admitting Zander's damaging lie detector testimony which included Zander's version of his post-examination conversation with the defendant.

The disputed conversation involved Wochnick's reaction to a display of knives, one of which was the knife removed from the victim's body. During the test, Zander had displayed five knives. Taking them one at a time, he'd laid them on the table in front of Wochnick and recorded his reaction. Wochnick's response to the first knife was normal. His response to the second knife, the murder weapon, was also normal. When Zander looked up, however, he saw that the defendant had his eyes closed. Zander said nothing but continued the test by tapping the table with his empty hand and asking his subject if he had seen this knife before. All reactions were normal.

Then Zander ordered the defendant to open his eyes and repeat the test. The reaction to the first knife was the same—normal. But when Wochnick looked at the blade that had been removed from the victim's body, said Zander, there was a violent change on the graph, indicating a guilty knowledge.

Technically, the test was finished at this point, but Zander asked yet another question: "Mr. Wochnick, if you can explain

these things to me—maybe you have a logical explanation.
Maybe you have a reaction you have not told me about. If you
can explain these things to me, I wish you would. Maybe the
whole thing is wrong."

According to the polygraphist, the defendant had then
replied, "Mr. Zander, I cannot explain that," thereby incriminating himself.

The Appellate Court decision recreated this conversation and
then commented:

> Defendant contends that by the introduction of the foregoing
> testimony under the guise of an accusatory statement, the
> prosecution was able to place in evidence the damaging and
> prejudicial results of the polygraph or so-called lie detector;
> that the results of such a test are not admissible as evidence
> and it was therefore prejudicial error to submit them indi-
> rectly in the form of a purported accusatory statement.

The court then pointed out that at this time "the question of
the admissibility in evidence of the results of the polygraph test
had not been decided in California." Various cases were cited,
after which the court continued, laying a basis for this final
conclusion:

> Respondent [the prosecution] argues that the results of the lie
> detector test were not placed before the jury; that the mere
> fact that the occasion for the conversation between defendant
> and a police officer was the giving of a lie detector test would
> not require the exclusion of such conversation if it were
> otherwise admissible and that moreover the trial court specif-
> ically instructed the jury it could not consider that portion of
> the conversation relating to the lie detector test as indicating
> whether or not there was any reaction to any technical test.
> Despite the instruction of the court, the evidence of the
> partial results of the test with respect to defendant's reaction
> upon being shown the murder weapon were indelibly im-
> planted in the minds of the jurors and could not have had a
> prejudicial effect.
> Not only was the evidence of the results of the lie detector
> test inadmissible but the testimony should have been rejected
> upon the further ground that it did not constitute an
> accusatory statement. The witness related that he told the

defendant some of the evidence had not been satisfactorily explained; that a number of questions had been asked as to his name and address and other questions of that nature which the machine inidcated he had answered truthfully but when certain other questions were put to him there was a violent reaction on the graph of the machine indicating the answers were untrue. . . .

Judgment and order reversed and cause remanded for a new trial.

Whatever satisfaction Wochnick may have enjoyed over his court victory and the prospect of a new trial was quickly dispelled. On September 22, 1950, a second jury found him guilty but reduced the charge from first degree murder to second, recommending that "he be punished by imprisonment in the state prison for the term prescribed by law." This meant a life sentence.

An Unsolved Murder

"**D**BF ... DBF ... DBF ..."

The alert came sputtering over the shortwave radio of Inspector Jay D. Downing's patrol car as he cruised along a quiet street in West Berkeley, California. A member of the Berkeley Police Department since 1954, Downing knew the seriousness of such a call, police code for "Dead Body Found." Eager for further instructions, he leaned forward to catch every word of information that would follow. Soon he was directed to an address only blocks away.

Arriving at a modest-looking apartment house on Sacramento Street, Inspector Downing was met by the building's owner and manager, who said he had found the brutally murdered victim in Apartment 1. The victim, who had lived in the apartment for some time, was known to the manager as Jim Mortin, a pleasant man about 28 years of age and a homosexual, employed by a local hospital to clean and otherwise care for delicate surgical instruments.

The building manager said he had entered the apartment with a passkey less than an hour earlier because Mortin, usually prompt in rent payments, was now weeks in arrears and had not been seen for a considerable time.

After a few minutes of further conversation, Inspector Downing asked for a passkey, explaining that he wanted to examine the apartment and view the body. Entering the rooms, he at once smelled the nauseating odor of decay. The sparsely furnished living room was clean and apparently undisturbed. In the bathroom washbasin lay a partially burned towel. A large smudge that looked like blood stood out on one of the walls.

Moving to the adjoining bedroom, Downing caught his first sight of the man's body. It was lying on the floor in a pool of blood. The left hand was stretched out with two pillows on it. Both head and body had been cruelly bludgeoned with a heavy metal skillet which lay on the floor nearby. The face was in a state of decomposition which accounted for the disturbing stench in the room. The body was clothed in a T-shirt and shorts.

The rear door of the kitchen was open, and Downing found an unwashed frying pan in the sink. It contained a small portion of meat, part of which had evidently been eaten by the victim or his assailant. In one corner of the kitchen stood a table with two chairs pushed under it and one shoved out.

Downing lost no time in sending for the coroner and calling headquarters for aides. He was instructed to take full charge of the case, an assignment that would extend to the end. Before long, half a dozen homicide detail men were on the scene with Downing. Together they began an inch-by-inch search of the entire apartment, hoping to find a tangible clue. Furniture, upholstery, and rugs were studied without result, and Downing undertook a scrupulous examination of walls and woodwork for fingerprints, using a high-powered magnifying glass.

Hours of work were finally rewarded when the inspector found a fingerprint carefully preserved on the bedroom door. To his delight, it was a clear impression—a print disclosing clearly defined loops and whorls.

Realizing the importance of his find, Inspector Downing summoned Captain Roland Sherry, in charge of records and identification, and asked him to come at once with all necessary supplies for copying what the inspector believed would prove to be one of the murderer's prints.

When Captain Sherry arrived, he quickly dusted the print and "lifted" it; he now had in his possession a precise reproduction of the fingerprint, which he could take back to the Bureau of

Identification and check with thousands of prints of known offenders. Before leaving, he took inked impressions of the dead man's fingertips, reasoning that if the victim had a police record it might provide a clue to the killer.

Meanwhile, Downing's search of the apartment revealed that someone, presumably the killer, had rifled the dresser drawers in the bedroom, leaving their contents in disarray. The detective surmised that whoever was guilty probably had been looking for articles or records that would reveal the dead man's past and associates. Downing also found rolls of undeveloped film which later proved to be pictures of a man identified by neighbors of the victim as a frequent visitor, a man they'd often heard addressed as Dan or Don.

Once back at headquarters, Captain Sherry began the difficult task of trying to match the lifted print and the impressions taken from the dead man's fingers. Hours passed without result, but Sherry was not a man to abandon so important a job. At last he hit pay dirt in both of his undertakings. First he further identified the murder victim, who had a record of frequent arrests on charges of lewd conduct. The name "Jim Mortin" had been an alias.

Detectives lost no time in visiting the hospital where the man had been employed, but their visit was fruitless. Mortin's superiors and associates could add little to what the police already knew. They referred to him as a peaceful, competent colleague who seemed to have a number of women friends.

When interviewed, these women spoke of Mortin as a dull, uninteresting person with religious interests, who was active in the affairs of his church.

Identification of the fingerprint lifted from the bedroom door was of greater importance. After Captain Sherry had compared it with many hundreds of recorded prints of known offenders, he concluded that they matched perfectly a print taken from a man arrested some time earlier for a minor offense. He was known under the alias George Billings, and the records showed he had been Mortin's roommate from 1959 to 1961. Tracing him to his present home was not difficult. The officers believed the mystery was just about solved.

When questioned, Billings emphatically denied any involvement in the murder. He insisted that he was under suspicion only because of his earlier trouble with the law. He did admit, as the police had already learned, that some years before he had occupied the same apartment in the same building. But he had moved after a short period of residence and could easily account for his whereabouts and movements since then.

Pursuing their investigation of Billings, detectives turned next to a reliable informer, a homosexual known to them as Tom. After listening to the facts, he offered several likely motives for the crime. He suggested that the victim might have brought home a homosexual and demanded money for a sex act, so angering the visitor that he turned killer. Tom explained that homosexuals detest "commercials," as male prostitutes are known among themselves.

Tom advanced still another possible motive, that perhaps the victim picked up someone who was not homosexual and been killed for making immoral advances. Tom then volunteered to accompany one of the detectives to Oakland and San Francisco to visit a number of gay bars and cafes, where they might learn something worthwhile.

Inspector R. B. Johnston was assigned to accompany Tom on a tour of the bars. Carrying police photographs of Mortin and Billings, they visited bar after bar without success. No one seemed to know either man.

When these efforts failed, the officers again turned to Billings, still suspecting that he was the guilty person. He was grilled again for hours with no success.

A few mornings later the homicide officers met to share their frustration and to plan further action. It was Inspector Downing who proposed the next move. "Why not give this man Billings a lie detector test?" he suggested.

"Is it worth the trouble?" one of the others inquired.

"Why not?" Downing shot back impatiently. "We've covered practically every moment of Billings' life since the hour estimated by the autopsy surgeon as the time of death. So now, what's wrong with trying the polygraph—if he's willing, of course?"

"But what about that fingerprint; doesn't that nail him to the murder?" interjected another officer. "I think we already have a perfect case against Billings."

Others nodded their agreement, but Downing still wasn't convinced.

Billings, who was not in technical custody but under orders to remain within call of the police, was sent for and informed of the proposal. To the surprise of everyone present, he was delighted. "You don't seem to believe me when I tell you I had nothing to do with that murder," he asserted. "Maybe you'll take my word for it if the lie detector says I'm telling the truth. Let's go ahead."

One of the department's most reliable polygraphists was telephoned and told to be prepared for an important test.

A short time later Downing and the suspect arrived at headquarters, and the examination proceeded in the usual way with pointed questions being reserved for the last.

"Did you kill that man in the apartment house where you formerly lived?" Billings was asked near the end of the examination.

"No—and on my word of honor."

Similar queries, rephrased, brought the same emphatic reply.

When the test was over, the polygraphist reported his certainty that the subject had spoken only the truth. The report amazed the police, who soon gathered again, wondering how next to proceed.

"What did he have to say about that fingerprint on the door?" someone asked the polygraphist, who was sitting with the group.

"He said it must be a very old one, but he couldn't explain its presence on the door," the lie detector expert replied. "A strange situation, but I'm positive he's truthful all the way. Personally, in connecting that print with your suspect I think you're barking up the wrong tree. Isn't there something else you can do to clear him?"

The question was a cue, and Captain Sherry caught it in an instant. "Our suspect tells us, as I recall, that this door was revarnished and repainted several times while he occupied that apartment," the Captain began. "If you'll allow me, I'd like to look into that."

"Go ahead," interjected Inspector Downing. "As far as I'm concerned, that door is yours. Do with it what you want."

Sherry eagerly accepted the challenge, and after the group had broken up he hastened to the telephone and called a carpenter.

Early the next morning they were in Mortin's bedroom. The door was carefully taken off its hinges, wrapped in cellophane, and transported to police headquarters where it was placed in a room with a "keep out" sign tacked to its entrance.

Then Captain Sherry went to work. Using a bottle of high-grade paint remover, an abrasive solution, and sheets of fine sandpaper, he began the arduous task of removing the paint and varnish, determined to do away with all of the old surface covering. What he wanted to know was what he would find on the original paint covering.

It was a tiring, trying job. He worked long into the night, scrubbing off the surfaces of new paint which Billings said had been applied. Obviously the door had been repainted at least four times.

As the police captain removed layer after layer, he found to his amazement that the fingerprint identified as Billings' remained almost unchanged and definitely in the same position. Even after he'd finished scraping the paint down to the original layer, the fingerprint remained. Inquiries to the apartment house manager brought the information that considerable time had elapsed since the door was first painted. Billings remembered having carelessly touched the wet paint while the initial coat was still wet. This had occurred while he was a tenant of the place—years before the murder.

How the original fingerprint could have remained so clear under these conditions provided a new mystery. Painters and paint dealers were consulted. They had only one answer—obviously an unusually high grade of paint had been used in renovating work over the years.

Police resourcefulness and hard work dispelled suspicions against Billings and verified the polygraphist's conclusion. In this case, exonerating an innocent suspect would have been impossible but for the ability of the polygraphist to distinguish truth from deception and to point the way toward further investigation.

Unfortunately, the murder has never been solved and the killer is still at large. But the polygraph helped save a man from being charged with a murder he did not commit.

A Judge Upholds Polygraphy

The perjury trial of Detective Sergeant Richard J. Ridling of the Detroit police has unusual legal significance. It set a new precedent, introduced by a federal judge, for the admission of lie detector evidence.

Ridling, with the support of his lawyers, had eagerly pleaded for a chance to vindicate himself with the aid of the polygraph. His earnestness finally won a favorable ruling for the defense in the U.S. District Court of Michigan. It was a decision that has since been widely quoted in legal quarters.

A cruel fate, however, deprived Ridling of the benefits of his victory. Because of ill health, the test he wanted so badly could not be made; and the accused police officer was obliged to face a jury without the polygraphic evidence he was certain would be in his favor. That he finally succeeded in proving his innocence before a jury is believed by many to have resulted in part from his avowed confidence that the lie detector would prove him innocent and his pleadings for such a test.

Detective Ridling's troubles began early in 1972 at the height of an official investigation of graft and corruption conducted by a federal grand jury. It was a sensational inquiry, culminating in the indictment of numerous police officers and civilians on charges of gambling conspiracy and bribery in what was described as a $40,000-a-day racket.

Ridling was one of many summoned to testify. He was strongly reluctant to appear as a witness, but a grand jury subpoena left him no recourse, especially since he had been promised immunity from prosecution for any self-incriminating statements he might make.

The key question put to Ridling by the grand jury was whether he had made contact with a notorious underworld figure at the Anchor Bar in Detroit. His answer, an unfortunate one for him, was "I can't recall."

The government prosecutor insisted that the reply had been "intentionally false." As a result, Ridling was indicted on a charge of perjury.

Considering himself innocent, the police officer engaged a well-known Detroit lawyer, Robert S. Harrison, to defend him. Before agreeing to become involved in the case, Harrison insisted on conducting his own investigation. With the aid of his partner and staff lawyers, Harrison succeeded in pinpointing the time and date of the controversial contact with the underworld figure and concluded that Ridling in fact had met that person as alleged by the government.

But Ridling, confronted with this information by the lawyer, had a ready explanation. He admitted that he now recalled the meeting but insisted that this fact had slipped his mind at the time he told the grand jurors he could not remember the incident. Hence, he argued that he had not committed perjury.

Harrison and his colleagues believed Ridling and they were determined to wage a vigorous fight in his behalf. At the outset, Harrison decided to use the lie detector. The man he chose to give the test was Lynn Marcy, whom he regarded as one of the foremost polygraphists in America. Marcy's examination of the accused was thorough, and he reported his conclusion that the accused policeman was speaking the truth. This judgment was brought to the attention of the authorities, who agreed to dismiss the indictment against Ridling. However, Ridling was subsequently reindicted on a similar perjury charge.

Attorney Harrison believed that Marcy, the polygraphist,

should be allowed to testify in Ridling's behalf, but the prosecutor took a different view. The defendant decided, therefore, to plead for a chance to face other examiners for verification of the initial findings. But the government lawyers objected to the proposal. Ridling and the defense appealed the case to the U.S. District Court, which ruled that testimony pertaining to new polygraph tests should be admissible evidence but subject to certain carefully defined conditions. The new examinations, stated Justice Charles W. Joiner, should be conducted under court supervision and should be conclusive, disclosing either that the subject was speaking the truth or lying.

This was a distinct departure from the frequently used stipulation procedure in which both sides participate in the selection of examiners and agree that the lie detector results, whether favorable or unfavorable to the defendant, be admitted in evidence. According to the new ruling, the judge himself would select the polygraphist. The decision, hailed by the accused and his counsel, caused a great deal of surprise in Michigan legal circles, primarily because of the justice's expressed confidence in the accuracy of polygraphy.

After carefully reviewing the basic aspects of the case, Justice Joiner wrote:

> Although polygraph testimony is sometimes referred to as experimental and scientific evidence, the evidence in reality is opinion evidence. The interrogation must be carefully arranged and supervised. The polygraph recordings must be interpreted. Only a person skilled in this art and science is qualified to interpret the results and interpretation is stated in the form of an opinion.
>
> At the beginning it must be noted that this among all possible cases, is the best case for testing the admissibility of polygraph testimony. A perjury case is based on 'willfully' or 'knowingly' giving false evidence. The experts all agree that the polygraph examination is aimed at exactly this aspect of truth. A subject, they say, may be honestly mistaken as to a fact and, if he answers according to his honest belief, the operator will interpret the results as being a truthful answer.
>
> There is in this country a reasonably well-developed group of persons who consider themselves to be experts in the use of the polygraph. They have recently organized into national and

state organizations to exchange ideas and to improve themselves. In some ways, they are looked down upon by members of the psychiatric and psychological societies.

In part, this comes from the limited educational background of many of the polygraph examiners and the mechanical and technical approach to their limited area of expertise. However, the scientific psychological basis for the polygraph examination is well established. . . .

Nothing, however, in the different techniques casts doubt upon the basic theory behind the polygraph. Experts assert that the record of one polygraph examination can be interpreted satisfactorily by another expert so long as that second expert knows the particular technique used in questioning the subject.

Commenting on the fact that "police departments throughout the United States, various parts of the government of the United States, and industry utilize polygraph test results in their day-to-day operations," he added:

Experts have testified that the reliability of the opinion of a reliable polygraph expert was greater than the opinions of ballistic experts and as high as the opinions of fingerprint experts.

In conclusion, Justice Joiner approached his final judgment by offering this unique landmark proposal for the admissibility of polygraph testimony in the case at bar. Its uniqueness should justify its repetition here:

The evidence of polygraph experts pertaining to the polygraph examination of the defendant and their opinions will be admitted subject to the following terms and conditions:

1. The parties will meet and will recommend to the court three competent polygraph experts other than those offered by the defendant.

2. The court will appoint one or more of the experts to conduct a polygraph examination.

3. The defendant shall submit himself for such examination at an appointed time.

4. The expert appointed by the court will conduct the examination and report the results to the court and to the counsel for both the defendant and the government.

5. If the results show, in the opinion of the expert, either that the defendant was telling the truth or that he was not telling the truth on the issues directly involved in this case, the testimony of the defendant's experts and the court's expert will be admitted.

6. If the tests indicate that the examiner cannot determine whether the defendant is or is not telling the truth, none of the polygraph evidence will be admitted.

7. In the event that the defendant declines to participate or cooperate in the test, none of the polygraph evidence will be admitted.

Both Attorney Harrison and his client read this proposal with keen satisfaction, but the prosecution took a different view. Especially annoyed was Lawrence Leff, director of the U.S. Justice Department's Organized Crime Strike Force in Detroit. Mr. Leff's objections to the proceedings were twofold. "We suspect the inherent reliability of the polygraph operator," he declared, "and we feel that admitting test results as evidence usurps the traditional role of the jury. If this were taken to its logical extension, there would be no need for a jury." Leff added that under the proposed procedure, trials would amount to no more than "a clash of polygraph experts."

Justice Joiner took sharp issue with this view, arguing that Leff's criticism reflected a misunderstanding of "how different juries are today than they were when the restrictive rules of evidence were first developed."

Both Ridling and his lawyer were elated when Justice Joiner named the celebrated John Reid of Chicago as his personally selected polygraphist. Reid first tested Ridling in Detroit and then later in the offices of the Reid Institute in Chicago. But to Ridling's dismay, the tests were inconclusive. In the many months that had passed between the initial trial and Joiner's opinion, Ridling had been stricken with ill health. He had developed diabetes as well as severe hypertension. Because of the impact of these maladies, Reid found himself unable to conduct an accurate test, and he reported this to the court.

Under the judge's proposal, there was no alternative but for Ridling to face a jury trial despite his eagerness for the lie detector procedure. Fate, however, was kind to him. After hearing Ridling tell his story on the stand and under oath but without hearing a word of polygraph testimony, the jurors returned a verdict of "Not guilty." Ridling was overjoyed, and Harrison was congratulated by everyone who had followed the intricacies of the trial.

Ridling's reinstatement as a working member of the Detroit Police Department followed quickly. He was also awarded back pay and full retroactive benefits.

The Forged Fingerprint

I f not for his blind faith in American justice and the dedication of a skilled investigator, William De Palma might not have retained his sanity during the two and a half years he occupied a narrow, dingy cell in McNeil Island Federal Penitentiary in Washington state, serving a term of fifteen years for a holdup he never committed.

That De Palma is free today and fully vindicated is due in great measure to the skill of Wilbur Lee Clingan, the former officer in charge of the Polygraph Section of the Los Angeles Police Department and now a member of the Pasadena force.

The crime for which De Palma was unjustly convicted occurred at noon on a warm November day in 1967 when a lone bandit with a gun walked up to a teller's counter in the Mercury Savings and Loan Society bank in Buena Park, California, and fled with $1,400 in a brown paper bag.

As detectives looked for clues, they found their lead on the teller's desk—the print of a left index finger. The print was found to belong to De Palma, who as a boy had been arrested—and fingerprinted—on a minor charge.

De Palma denied the bank robbery accusation, explaining that at the time of the robbery he had been eleven miles from the bank selling sandwiches and coffee from his catering wagon. But his denials carried little weight despite the testimony of thirteen people who swore in court that at the time of the crime they were buying food from him just as he claimed.

Although he was defended by an able lawyer, De Palma's alibi failed to impress the jury at his trial, probably because of damning expert testimony about the fingerprint.

The jury found De Palma guilty, and he was sentenced to fifteen years in the federal prison. An appeal was filed at once, and while awaiting a decision the accused man, free on bail, tried to find someone who would assume the difficult task of proving his innocence.

After a number of people had turned deaf ears to his pleas, De Palma telephoned the criminology departments of various Southern California universities in search of a person who could help him. He explained that imprisonment would leave his wife and three daughters destitute. Nevertheless, his appeals brought no assistance. He had been told by a spokesman for the Orange County's public defender office that this department could not help because De Palma was accused of a federal offense.

In desperation, De Palma continued his efforts to find aid and finally heard about an astute private detective named John Bond, a former investigator for the county's public defender.

"In spite of all the government's witnesses," the accused man told Bond when they first met, "I swear that I had nothing to do with that holdup. I was miles away. And that fingerprint they found on the counter wasn't made by me. Still, I'm a convicted man facing prison. What can you do to help me?"

Bond, known as a tenacious fighter for justice as well as a resourceful investigator, replied that he would like to assist but that De Palma must first undergo a lie detector test. "If it proves you to be truthful," said Bond, "I'll take your case and do my level best."

De Palma, who was more than willing to take the test, asked who would administer it.

"Only one man," Bond replied. "His name is Wilbur Lee Clingan, and he retired from the Los Angeles force a time ago. If he tests you and finds that you're truthful, I'll do everything in the world for you—or else. You know, no one ever came to me and said he was guilty. I'm in business to help innocent people."

De Palma lost no time contacting Clingan, and an appointment was made for a lie detector test. It lasted close to four hours, and as soon as it ended, the polygraphist called Bond. "De Palma didn't rob that bank," he told the investigator. "Of that I'm positive. I'm convinced now that he's never been in that bank in his life."

The report from the man he trusted satisfied Bond. He decided to take the case even though it would bring him a ridiculously low fee, for De Palma had spent all of his money on his defense and was $10,000 in debt. Money, however, meant nothing to Bond when justice was at stake.

First Bond was eager to gather all the available facts. Bond knew that De Palma had been positively identified as the robber by two women tellers at the bank; that a police department fingerprint expert had testified that the fingerprint taken from the counter definitely belonged to the accused; and that a second police expert had verified the fingerprint testimony.

To offset such damaging evidence, the defense had only the alibi statements of the witnesses who swore that at the time of the robbery De Palma was miles away selling them food.

Puzzled by this apparent imbalance in the weight of evidence, Bond realized that he must in some way account for such a conflict. Launching an investigation of his own, he started checking with merchants near the bank and found a woman who insisted that De Palma answered a description of the bandit as provided by bank employees. However, when she looked at a photograph of the convicted man, she shook her head and admitted that he was not the man she had seen.

Bond went to a newspaper morgue and asked to see clippings on every bank robbery committed in the area in the past three years. He discussed these with seasoned detectives, reasoning that the Buena Park holdup might have been committed by a discharged offender. Inquiries led to a man recently discharged from prison, but this person said that although he had committed twenty-five holdups, he was innocent of this one. "If I'd pulled that one, I'd tell you," he said. "Right now I've got nothing to lose."

After more time spent on investigative work of this sort, the thoroughly frustrated Bond felt obliged to report his failures to his client. "Please don't stop," De Palma pleaded. "I've got no one else; maybe I'll get a new trial after all."

However, De Palma was due for disappointment. In February 1971, Judge Charles Carr handed down a decision refusing a retrial. "A judge," he ruled, "has no desire to see an innocent man convicted. I've wanted to be as nearly sure as I can in this case. Frankly, it's the fingerprint that did the job."

Both Bond and De Palma realized the significance of this last comment, but there appeared to be nothing they could do. If they could disprove the print's authenticity, they might have a chance, but they had no idea of how to do that.

Finally the accused man's stay of execution, previously extended by the court to allow more time for investigation, expired. It was now August 1971, and one morning two deputy U.S. marshals called on De Palma to tell him that he must go to prison. It was a crushing blow. Shortly afterward, he accompanied the federal officers on the 1,200-mile trip to the island penitentiary.

Recalling that experience years later, De Palma told of his feelings on the torturous journey. "I loved my country," he related, "I believed in law and order, and suddenly everything I believed in put me in a penitentiary and tore my family to pieces."

In a cell with nine other men. De Palma feared that he would go berserk. Day and night he was haunted by visions of his wife and daughters, now living without him and without funds. He feared physical violence; once he was obliged to defend himself against a crazed prisoner.

Only prayer and hope helped him in his determination to fight off insanity. He wrote constantly to Bond, but the investigator's replies were not encouraging. The prisoner's wife, Marie, wrote that the welfare department had allocated the family only $260 a month. Mrs. De Palma was trying her best to keep up morale; she was urging the girls to do well in school. Good marks, she told them, "would make Daddy happy."

On the outside, Bond continued his futile effots to solve the mystery of the damning fingerprint, asking many experts for advice. At last he interviewed a former Buena Park policeman who offered new hope.

"Strange things happen with fingerprints," the retired officer told him, recalling an old case of a holdup in which a gun had been found close to the robbery scene. He had dusted the revolver for prints and found none. Weeks later, another policeman, who pretended to be a fingerprint expert, told the authorities that he had discovered three prints on the weapon and all of them matched those of suspects jailed for the robbery.

"It's almost unexplainable," said Bond's informant. "I knew there couldn't be a fingerprint on that gun, and I was certain that some funny business had occurred. You know—or you should know—that prints can be transplanted or forged by someone willing to be corrupt."

Bond consulted police authorities and the district attorney, who assigned the case to two crime laboratory technicians, Larry Ragle and Robert Wagener. Specifically, they were called on to determine whether the fingerprint that had been introduced in evidence could be a forgery.

Ragle and Wagener began by examining the fingerprint under a powerful microscope, and it was not long before they made a startling discovery. The particles of the dusting powder on the two prints were widely different; only the powder on one print resembled that used by the Buena Park police. Powder on the old print resembled that which is used in Xerox copying machines. It was obvious to the two officers that the bank print had been forged. They hastened to inform Bond of their conclusion.

Bond went to the island prison to share the news with De Palma. "My God," exclaimed the convict, "why do you suppose this was done to me?"

Bond could only shrug his shoulders. "Perhaps," he reasoned, "someone thought you were guilty and wanted to make sure of your conviction."

De Palma, still in custody, was brought before Judge Carr in February 1974, and the prosecution moved that the indictment against him be dismissed. The motion was granted, and De Palma left the courtroom a free and happy man.

PART THREE

In Conclusion

26

Congress Probes the Polygraph

In recent years some members of Congress have bitterly protested the current practice of requiring applicants for employment in federal government agencies to take lie detector tests.

Seven bills to outlaw this practice have been introduced in the House of Representatives; the latest was sponsored by Bella S. Abzug, then a Democrat representative from Manhattan. In announcing the introduction of her measure (H.R.131917), she declared that she had received communications from the Central Intelligence Agency, the Defense and Treasury Departments, the Federal Reserve Board, and the Postal Service upholding the use of the polygraph for various purposes, mostly for screening job applicants.

Representative Abzug added that the CIA disclosed that more than 60 percent of its job applicants rejected on security grounds from 1963 through mid-1974 were turned down on the basis of lie detector interviews. In voicing vigorous objection to this, the New York congresswoman asserted that "the polygraph cannot distinguish truth from falsehood." Her bill, now before the House, would make it a criminal offense to administer polygraph tests in connection with jobs in the federal government. The bill would also apply to private employers involved in interstate commerce or dealing with the government. It would not, however, affect the use of the polygraph in criminal investigations.

Representative Abzug, in an interview, quoted CIA director George Bush as saying that about half of the agency's job applicants who were rejected because of polygraph test information "had already completed all other necessary screening and been provisionally approved on this basis."

Bush, she stated, had written her a letter which argued, ". . . it is reasonable to assume that the program is a significant deterrent to application for employment by unsuitable candidates, and more importantly, penetration attempts by foreign intelligence services."

Bush also said that his agency had "adopted strict procedures to prevent abuses," which included notifying each applicant about the use of polygraph tests, warning that a privilege against self-incrimination exists, and limiting questions to "security issues."

In a letter to Mrs. Abzug, Assistant Secretary of Defense Terence McClary stated that the Defense Department had moved to upgrade the polygraph program over the last few years and had adopted limitations "to insure the protection of rights of all individuals." He added that a new "objective assessment of its utility in the investigative process" was under way.

Speaking for the Treasury Department, Assistant Secretary for Enforcement Operations and Traffic Affairs David R. Mac-Donald claimed, "The polygraph is used sparingly by Treasury Enforcement agencies as one among many investigative techniques, but it is not a general exploratory mechanism."

Arthur F. Burns, chairman of the Federal Reserve Board, said that polygraph tests were given to employees of four Federal Reserve Banks last year, all in cases involving criminal larceny. Most of them, he explained, were conducted "at the suggestion of or with the concurrence of the Federal Bureau of Investigation." In Burns' opinion, polygraph devices should not be used to screen applicants or for other personnel inquiries.

Speaking for his department, Postmaster General Benjamin F. Bailer explained that the Postal Inspection Services uses polygraph tests "in some criminal investigations to narrow a list of suspects after other investigative methods have failed." The greatest benefit, he said, was in vindicating innocent employees. All tests, he added, were on a voluntary basis.

According to Mrs. Abzug, the Justice Department "consistently opposes the admission of polygraph evidence at trials." The department, she asserted, had sent her no substantive reply or acknowledgment to her inquiries regarding the lie detector. She added that government agencies using the polygraph also include the Customs Service, the Drug Enforcement Administration, and the FBI. She estimated that fully 200,000 people undergo polygraph tests annually in pre-employment or employment situations. The bill she proposed would make the use of lie detectors in such cases a misdemeanor punishable by a fine of $1,000 and would permit suits in federal court for damages. Mrs. Abzug's proposed legislation, along with four similar measures, has been referred to the House Judiciary Committee.

Congressional concern over the lie detector's accuracy and legality actually began well before the introduction of these bills. For two busy days in 1974, a parade of personally interested citizens both for and against the polygraph testified before the Subcommittee of the Committee on Government Operations of the House of Representatives to voice their views on the subject.

Some praised the lie detector as a reliable, indispensable instrument in crime detection and industry; others branded it as inaccurate and unworthy of use. In sum, the minutes of the hearing provided a veritable encyclopedia on the subject and its history. The committee reached no conclusions, nor were any specific cases involving use of the polygraph cited. However, the two-day hearings brought out a wide diversity of views which will undoubtedly influence congressional action on pending measures.

The end result of the hearings was the publication of a 790-page report printed by the government. A review of so lengthy a document here must necessarily be brief and confined to only the most important highlights.

Chairing the hearings was Representative William S. Moorhead of Pennsylvania, chairman of the Foreign Operations and Government Information Subcommittee.

The committee spared no effort to hear all sides of the issue, listening to many who were technically and professionally interested in lie detector operations, including heads of institutions devoted to polygraph services and law enforcement agencies as well as spokesmen for such liberal organizations as the American Civil Liberties Union, who believe that use of the polygraph is unconstitutional and therefore illegal as an invasion of the individual rights and security of American citizens.

In opening the hearings, Chairman Moorhead sought to clarify their purpose with this statement:

> This series of investigative hearings into the use of the so-called lie detection and telephone monitoring devices by the federal government has a twofold purpose:
>
> First, the last hearings on these subjects were conducted a decade ago, and Congress needs to know whether federal agencies have increased or decreased their use. . . .
>
> Second, over the past several years, technological changes have occurred in both fields which have grave implications on the question of invasion of privacy. It is time to look at these developments; what we want to know is exactly where we stand now. In my view, the nation is getting extremely impatient over the whole question of invasion of privacy and snooping by the government regardless of how well-meaning such practices might be.

The first witness sworn was Robert E. Smith, associate director of the Project on Privacy and Data Collection of the American Civil Liberties Union Foundation and vigorous opponent of the polygraph, who stated:

> The polygraph machine used as a so-called lie detector, I think, essentially raises privacy issues. It is our belief that no person should be required, by moral or legal compulsion, to submit to a lie detector test. The courts have found that the Bill of Rights taken as a whole constitutes a right to privacy, and it is this combination of rights too that is violated by use of polygraph testing.

Richard C. Arthur, a polygraph industry expert, followed with this sharply worded, contrary view:

> The results of properly administered polygraph examinations

are very accurate. The latest estimate based on a five-year study of those persons tested by the senior author accords to his polygraph technique an accuracy of over 96 percent with a 3 percent margin of inconclusive determinations, and a one percent margin of maximum possible error.

The Committee, in its exhaustive report, turned next to lie detector evaluation in foreign countries, quoting Professor Alan Westin:

In Europe, the courts, legal codes, and authoritative commentators have long rejected the lie detector as an impermissible police technique, not on the ground of its error ratio but because it is felt to violate the essential dignity of the human personality and individuality of the citizen. It was this formulation of the issue that led Pope Pius XII in 1958 to condemn the lie detector.

The report then turned to far earlier attempts to regulate use of the polygraph at federal, state, and local levels of government:

One of the earliest attempts occurred in 1952, when a proposal was made in the House of Representatives to investigate government use of polygraphs and to determine if employees needed legislative protection. . . .
In its survey of 58 federal agencies, the Moss Commission discovered that 19 of them, including the CIA and NRA, had conducted 19,796 tests during 1963.

The report went on to say that after seven days of public hearings, the Moss Commission had concluded:

There is no lie detector, neither machine nor human. People have been deceived by a myth that a metal box in the hands of an investigator can detect truth or falsehood.

The Committee also gave its attention to various attempts to regulate polygraph tests. It cited a New Jersey law enacted in 1956, which provided that "any person who as an employer shall influence, request, or require any employee to take or submit to a lie detector test as a condition of employment or continued employment is a disorderly person." In that state an individual declared "a disorderly person" is subject to a maximum fine of $1,000 and/or a term of up to one year in prison.

Opposing such legislation, John Macy, chairman of the Civil Service Commission, told the committee he believed there was no need for such measures to protect federal employees. The agencies themselves, he contended, are capable of protecting their workers.

Attention was given to an adverse finding of the Warren Commission with this statement:

> In evaluating the polygraph, due consideration must be given to the fact that a psychological response may be caused by factors other than deception, such as fear, anxiety, neurosis, dislike, and other emotions. There are no valid statistics as to the reliability of the polygraph. . . .

Strongly contradicting this conclusion was the reported testimony of J. Kirk Barefoot, chairman of the Legislative and Law Committee of the American Polygraph Association, who argued:

> The objectives of our association shall be the advance of the use of the polygraph as a profession as a means of promoting social welfare, the encouragement of the use of the polygraph in its broadest and most liberal manner by promotion of research into instrumentation and techniques.

The speaker was followed on the stand by the association's general counsel, Charles Marino of Chicago, who dwelt heavily on what he referred to as the recent trend of courts toward leniency in recognizing polygraph evidence under stipulated conditions. He concluded:

> . . . there are a growing number of court cases each year in which the results of polygraph examinations are being recognized as admissible in evidence under certain circumstances and provided a proper foundation is laid. I expect that this pattern will continue in the future.

Much emphasis was laid on the intensive training of polygraph examiners throughout the country. Attention was also given to the use of the lie detector by the FBI, which was said to maintain forty-three pieces of polygraph equipment used by thirty-nine trained agents operating in thirty-six field offices.

Considerable time was spent listening to military spokesmen who detailed the training of polygraph examiners in the Military Police School at Fort Gordon, Georgia. Since 1951, it was explained, the Army has trained 1,251 polygraph examiners. The training program is for the benefit of the Army, the Air Force, the Navy, Marine Corps, Treasury and Postal Service.

One of the most severe blows dealt the polygraph in the entire two-day hearing came from Stefan T. Possony, writing to Chairman Moorhead for the Hoover Foundation on War, Revolution, and Peace at Stanford University in California:

> A perusal of the data submitted to your Committee convinces me that the scientific efforts devoted to polygraph matters could easily rank as the worst program sponsored by the government. . . .
>
> In spite of my skepticism, I always believed that the polygraph machines would be working with top reliability. Now it turns out that the machines and the maintenance procedures are defective and that my optimism was naïve. I am sorry to say that lack of care must reflect on the professionals. . . .
>
> I note the recurrent argument that the polygraph—because it has so many defects—should be used only on personnel engaged in national security affairs, intelligence, and counterintelligence. My own logic tells me that if the polygraph is unreliable or invalid, or at any rate, has not been proved to be valid, it should not be used on security and intelligence personnel either. What's the point in getting undependable answers and in practicing machine-fabricated self-deception? One does not utilize bad aircraft to fly the most important missions; such missions are flown with the best aircraft that can be designed. This same philosophy needs to be applied to the fields where the polygraph could be relevant. . . .

Possony's letter concludes with this unusual recommendation:

> At a recent conference in Prague a rumor was circulated that the Communists are at work on a mind-control technology having a range of up to fifty miles. This may have been so much propaganda, but I learned from a independent ex-Soviet source that for many years there has been functioning in Moscow an institute which is researching thought-control methods for military purposes.
>
> We might as well recognize that while we are fiddling on a very squeaky instrument, the Soviets may be doing serious and forward-looking work.

Polygraphy in the Armed Forces

In the face of congressional efforts to ban the use of lie detector tests on personnel in federal government agencies as a condition of employment or promotion, it is interesting to note that the Army, Navy, Air Force, and Marines still use the polygraph in investigative work. These services prescribe rules for lie detector examinations that call for the utmost care in defending the individual rights of its personnel. Not only are military personnel protected from mandatory lie detector tests, but a high quality of perfection and expertise is required of those trained by the military for polygraph examinations.

Each Army post in the United States maintains a staff of well-trained polygraphists whose services are frequently used in investigating charges of theft, immorality, and unmilitary-like conduct. Polygraphy also plays its part in the investigating of war crimes.

Not long ago, for example, in the San Francisco Presidio, a long-established military reservation, a soldier of low rank faced a court martial on a charge of rape against the wife of a high Army officer.

While the soldier admitted having had sexual relations with the woman, he denied the rape accusation, insisting that his actions had her consent and were without force. The woman strongly denied this, claiming that he had used force and acted against her will and desires. Both were subjected to lie detector tests, which the examiner regarded as inconclusive. Graphs indicated that both, in measure, were speaking the truth in recounting their conflicting stories, and the polygraphist conceded that he could not determine which party was lying. In view of this, the charges were dropped and there was no court martial.

Although many civilian lawyers believe that the military's rules for use of the lie detector are more protective of civil rights than laws concerning lie detector tests of civilians, military lawyers contend that there is little if any difference in the nature or protective value of the military regulations.

Establishing a general policy on conditions under which use of the lie detector is justified, military regulations prescribe:

The investigation by other means [than polygraph] must have been as thorough as circumstances permit, the subject [must have] been interviewed, and consistent with the circumstances of the case, the development of additional information by means of the polygraph [must be] essential and timely for the further conduct of the investigation.

There is reasonable cause to believe that the person to be examined has knowledge of, or was involved in, the matter under investigation.

It is the policy of the Department of the Army that criminal and counterintelligence investigations, to include personal security investigations, be oriented to depend upon evidence secured through skillful investigations and interrogation rather than upon the possibility of self-disclosure by a polygraph examination.

The probing of a person's thoughts or beliefs and questions about conduct which have no security implications or are not directly relevant to the investigation is prohibited. Examples of subject area which should not be probed unless directly relevant include the following: religious beliefs and affiliations, beliefs and opinions regarding racial matters, political beliefs and affiliations of a nonsubversive nature, and opinions regarding the constitutionality of legislative policies.

To protect those refusing to be tested, the regulations read:

Adverse action shall not be taken against a person for refusal to take a polygraph examination or for unwillingness to volunteer to take a polygraph examination. Further, information concerning a person's refusal to submit to a polygraph examination shall not be recorded in any personal files. . . .

Not every Army officer of high rank can authorize use of the lie detector, for the regulations carry this restriction:

No polygraph examination shall be conducted without the authorization of the Commanding General of the U.S. Continental Army Command, general overseas commands, separate task forces, heads of Army staff agencies with an assigned criminal investigation polygraph capacity, commanding officer U.S. Army of CID [Criminal Investigation Division] agency, or superintendents of U.S. Military Academy or their designated representatives. . . .

The conduct of such examinations is carefully defined with these specific restrictions:

A polygraph examination will not be conducted unless the person to be examined has been advised that he has a right to consult with a lawyer or to have a lawyer present to observe the examination, whether the area in which the polygraph examination is to be conducted contains a two-way mirror or other device whereby the examinee can be observed without his knowledge, and whether the examination will be monitored in whole or in part by any means. . . . Polygraph examination shall be conducted only by personnel certified as polygraph examiners in accordance with this regulation. . . . Polygraph examiner trainees serving their apprenticeship will conduct polygraph examinations only under the direct supervision of a certified polygraph examiner.

This is followed by special provisions that no such examinations will be conducted when in the judgment of the examiner the subject is "mentally or physically fatigued . . . obviously unduly emotionally upset, intoxicated, or under the influence of narcotics, marijuana, or dangerous drugs or the examiner is known to be addicted to narcotics or to have a mental disorder." The examiner also faces these sharp orders:

Prior to the beginning of each test the examiner will review with the examinee all questions to be asked during the test; under no circumstances will polygraph examiners allow themselves to be identified as other than investigative personnel. Polygraph examiners will not wear white coats or similar items of clothing which might create a clinical appearance. . . .

Polygraph examiners will not participate in any public demonstration of the polygraph technique that includes a mock test in which there is any attempt to interpret the results of the test.

The confidentiality of polygraph examination reports is scrupulously guarded as follows:

Such results are not to be made available outside of the Department of the Army excepting that they may go to officials of the Office of the Secretary of Defense . . . other federal officials charged with intelligence, security, or law enforcement responsibilities with a clear need to know . . . state law enforcement officials where the results indicate an alleged violation of state law or that a serious crime is likely to be committed.

In another paragraph the rights of suspects or accused persons to undergo polygraph examinations for self-vindication are carefully set forth. They include the following:

Nothing in this regulation shall preclude the conduct of a polygraph examination when an individual under investigation or association with an investigation voluntarily seeks a polygraph examination as a means of exculpation. All such voluntary requests shall be reviewed . . . to determine the propriety of the request and to assure compliance with other requirements of this regulation.

Such is the Army's concept of criminal justice within its ranks.

CHAPTER
28

A Look Into the Future

Will a vastly expanded use of the lie detector curb today's shocking rise of crime and violence in America? Can the lie detector, applied to applicants for parole and probation, convert our prisons into places of rehabilitation rather than punitive institutions? Can the polygraph probe the innermost thoughts and emotions of convicts to determine whether they are ready to return to a law abiding society as safe, self-reliant citizens?

Two well-known California polygraphists subscribe to such a program and firmly advocate its trial in their state. They have written their views in a comprehensive, widely-discussed brochure entitled *A New Approach to the Rehabilitation of Convicted Criminals*. The authors are George W. Harman, head of a polygraph company based in San Francisco with branches in various other cities; and his former partner Herbert Johnson, who still practices his profession in the West. Both are members of the American Polygraph Association and of the California Association of Polygraph Examiners.

Harman and Johnson's plans have the endorsement of many professionals in the field, including Clinton T. Duffy, one of the most highly regarded penologists in the country and the former warden of San Quentin Penitentiary. According to Duffy, "This program could possibly be one of the most effective therapeutic experiences of their [the offenders] lifetime."

Harman and Johnson introduce their subject with a bitter attack on the American prison system of today, a system which they claim results in a startlingly high rate of recidivism and fails to turn the onetime offender onto lawful paths in a free society. They cite statistics to show that although a recent poll revealed that 75 percent of Americans favor rehabilitation as the prison goal, the present system of corrections in this country has failed to bring about the rehabilitation of many offenders. They point to a study disclosing that of 18,833 men and women released from the federal criminal justice system in a single year, 11,477 were rearrested a number of times. Of those freed on probation 55 percent committed new crimes, while 61 percent of those released on parole committed new crimes compared with 74 percent who had returned to crime after serving their complete sentences.

A prison record itself is a hindrance to rehabilitation, say Harman and Johnson, since too few employers will hire an ex-convict. In support, they refer to a popular poll showing that 42 percent of the public would hesitate to hire, even as a janitor, a former robber who had shot someone; 75 percent would not hire him as a clerk handling money.

Facing these statistics, Harman and Johnson consider a number of alternatives, one of which calls for more punitive measures in prisons; another which proposes an increase in detection forces, which in their opinion merely means apprehending more criminals. A third proposal, they say, demands an increase in jail facilities—a move which they believe would simply reinforce the existing problem. A fourth alternative demands an increased number of probation and parole officers, a solution which the authors regard as ineffective and unworthy, explaining:

An increase in the number of probation and parole officers, as with an increase in prisons, would not necessarily mitigate the problems of the system and could perpetuate them. It is the prison system itself which makes the rehabilitation of offenders so difficult, and it is the prison system which must be modified to ease the burden of the probation and parole officer. Until a more effective way of rehabilitating offenders is implemented, the problems will not lessen.

As a fifth alternative the writers turn to the effective use of polygraphy in private industry and in business as a means of detecting theft and preventing it:

> Many private firms presently utilize the services of polygraphists in screening prospective employees in order to prevent further problems. It is not uncommon for a polygraphist who has been consulted for a specific theft or a problem of high inventory losses to find a great number of other employees involved in pilferage of varying degrees. According to many of these employees they stole to avoid the social ostracism of fellow employees. For reasons which are obvious, stealing employees would not trust those who would not participate in these activities. It is not uncommon in such cases for the firm to disregard past stealing with the stipulation that periodic polygraph tests be made to eliminate stealing in the future. Because these employees know that future unfavorable tests would bring about their termination, they are deterred significantly from stealing.

According to Harman and Johnson, the need of conscience by the individual—or lack of it—frequently accounts for the failure of rehabilitation efforts. It would be through the use of the polygraph as a "substitute conscience" that the rehabilitation of offenders would be realized:

> Prisons are an educational experience in themselves, training criminals to be more effective in committing crime. These efforts are based on the assumption that the new crime will be successful. The use of the polygraph as a requirement for release would contradict this kind of thinking and provide certainty about the detection of the future criminal activity. . . .
> The opportunity to specify periodic polygraph examination offers the judge another alternative to placing a man in a penal institution. With this means of detection at his disposal, the judge could become more confident in granting probation; that is, in borderline cases the deterrent effect of the polygraph examination would provide the assurance needed to grant probation rather than impose a prison sentence.

The authors maintain that because the convicted person could choose either to accept or refuse the polygraph examination as a requisite to probation, there would be no infringement of Constitutional rights.

Here the authors come to the nub of their discussion, proposing a pilot program for California utilizing the lie detector as previously mentioned. Their proposal should be told in their own words:

> It is proposed here that a four-year program be established in California in which a full-time private professional polygraph corporation would administer polygraph tests to probation and parole candidates. . . . The use of a private polygraphist is essential, for this would separate this method of rehabilitation from the traditional criminal justice agencies. . . .
>
> Furthermore the probation or parole officer would be free to concentrate more on a therapeutic relationship with the client. In developing rapport with his client, the probation and parole officer would be assured of his client's sincerity. Emphasis would be changed from supervision to treatment. . . .
>
> It is not proposed that the polygraph examiners be probation and parole officers. They would be an aid to the probation and parole officers, and would be involved only in determining the truthfulness of the candidates. The polygraphist, for example, would not decide what constituted a violation of probation or parole, nor would he be involved in deciding what disposition would be made in cases where violations are discovered ... polygraphists have found that, because of the certainty of polygraph results, some individuals lose all inhibition when confronted with the polygraph. They suddenly relate to the examiners quite openly about their dishonest activities and these confessions provide them with a tremendous sense of relief. . . .

Pertinent to such a plan, Harman and Johnson point out, is the matter of cost to the state—and that means to the taxpayer. They assert that the average annual cost for incarcerating a juvenile offender in California is $5,626 compared with $5,777 for an adult. The cost increases for recidivists. The community and the offender, according to the writers, are better off socially and financially if the offender can be released on probation rather than being sent to prison, so that from a purely financial standpoint, the community benefits from the probation system.

Summarizing their unique and somewhat revolutionary proposal, Harman and Johnson state:

> We propose that a four-year pilot program be established so that meaningful statistics and the fruits of continuing research can be compiled to show not only the cost effectiveness of the program, but also a significant reduction in probation violations and in the amount of 'repeat' crimes by persons who had previously been convicted of crime. . . .
>
> The reduction, we feel, will be a reduction in crime rates, a significant reduction in cost because of crime in California, and a meaningful increase in the rehabilitation effect of the California criminal justice system. . . .
>
> The authors believe that this program, given a long-term chance to prove itself, will have a definite and profound effect in abating crime within the community, rehabilitating offenders, and lessening our crowded court calendars, all of which will work to the advantage of everyone concerned.

The philosophy and working program of much of Harman and Johnson's plan are being followed today in the state of Oregon with gratifying results, according to Lieutenant L. T. Riegel of the Department of State Police of Oregon. Detailing his current program (which does not include parolees), Lieutenant Riegel writes:

> We do not give the examination [lie detector] as a condition of getting probation. Rather it is a continuing examination every sixty days, sooner if necessary, to retain their probation granted by the court. The examination encompasses abstaining from all law violations; seeking, obtaining, and retaining employment; disassociation with other criminal acts or those engaged in criminal activity, both present or past; nonuse of drugs or intoxicants in excess of that permitted within the probation regulations; and being truthful in oral interviews and written reports to their probation officer.
>
> The polygraph examination does not take the place of oral and written reporting by the probationer to his probation officer. Instead it aids the officer in determining if the information he has received is factual. It also is a good indicator if a probationer is slipping before it actually becomes so gross that the court must revoke the probation. We have

been successful in pulling several back into limits and keeping them on the job and their family off the welfare rolls.

I believe it is only fair to explain that the only ones placed on this experimental program are those with extensive records having failed at probation on previous occasions who would have definitely received a prison sentence had they not agreed to participate in the program.

Our successes are not outstanding until some thought is given to the type of man and the statistics showing that his changes or probation success are less than 15 percent on regular probation. Our percentage is better than 50 percent on those starting the program and remaining until their probation period is completed or their charts become clean and attitude is such that we can recommend to the court that they be placed on an indefinite time before the next examination.

Some are held in an inactive position. Some have progressed sufficiently to be completely discharged from the program in advance of the completion of the program.

It is quite gratifying to see men, forty to fifty years of age, who are now working, drawing pay checks for the first time in their lives.

Our program is a test program with a limited number, approximately one hundred, and we have hopes of building sufficient statistics to allow other departments to support a polygraph examiner and this type of program.

Only time and trial will adequately evaluate the Riegel program and other advances, but sociologists and criminologists agree that over the years practical use of the lie detector in the administration of criminal justice represents an important forward step in providing justice to the accused. They point to the great Hans Gross' assertion that the quest for exact truth is the root of all effective crime detection. The cases detailed here obviously verify Gross' sound belief. And yet one may wonder whether Gross had been originally inspired by the words of the ancient Jewish sages—"Truth is the heart of life."

Index